"Antoine Gendre used the subprime crisis as an opportunity to relocate families in need of a house with a strong return on investment for investors. He was able to bring to the surface the Section 8 program, allowing tenants to have subsidies and the investor to obtain high returns thanks to entering at entry-level real estate prices. As a financial advisor, my European clients have been happy to contribute to the recovery of the real estate market in the United States and obtain returns higher than any other investment channel available to them."

—Franck Nogues,
onseils & Patrimoines

"When I met Antoine, I was exposed to the world of Section 8 from an investor's viewpoint, and it has transformed the way I invest in real estate. His vast experience and knowledge of Section 8 was extremely helpful in helping me launch my real estate investment company to the next level. I attribute much of my success with Section 8 investments to Antoine's mastery on the subject."

—Marcelo Gomez,
personal injury attorney

"I admire people that can make a complex concept simple. I admire Antoine Gendre. He has made Section 8 investing simple to comprehend in his book Cash Flow from Day One."

—Gary Sirak,
author of The American Dream Revisited

CA$H
FLOW
FROM DAY 1

CA$H FLOW

FLOW

FROM DAY 1

THE ULTIMATE GUIDE TO
GETTING MORE FROM AMERICAN REAL ESTATE
RIGHT FROM YOUR LIVING ROOM

ANTOINE GENDRE

Published by Advantage, Charleston, South Carolina.
Member of Advantage Media Group.

ADVANTAGE is a registered trademark, and the Advantage colophon is a trademark of Advantage Media Group, Inc.

Printed in the United States of America.

ISBN: 978-1-59932-646-7
LCCN: 2016933923

This publication is designed to provide accurate and authoritative information in regard to the subject matter covered. It is sold with the understanding that the publisher is not engaged in rendering legal, accounting, or other professional services. If legal advice or other expert assistance is required, the services of a competent professional person should be sought.

Advantage Media Group is proud to be a part of the Tree Neutral® program. Tree Neutral offsets the number of trees consumed in the production and printing of this book by taking proactive steps such as planting trees in direct proportion to the number of trees used to print books. To learn more about Tree Neutral, please visit **www.treeneutral.com.** To learn more about Advantage's commitment to being a responsible steward of the environment, please visit **www.advantagefamily.com/green**

Advantage Media Group is a publisher of business, self-improvement, and professional development books and online learning. We help entrepreneurs, business leaders, and professionals share their Stories, Passion, and Knowledge to help others Learn & Grow. Do you have a manuscript or book idea that you would like us to consider for publishing? Please visit **advantagefamily.com** or call **1.866.775.1696.**

The dedication of this book is split in three ways:

To Paul,
To Strategic Coach,
To those who believe in the American dream.

TABLE OF CONTENTS

INTRODUCTION:
A BETTER INVESTMENT

These days, traditional investment channels provide a return on investment of less than 5 percent. For some investors, that may seem like a pretty good number. But what if I told you that there is a way to experience two or three times that return in the real estate space?

This book is about being a different kind of investor or real estate business entrepreneur—someone who thinks outside the box and is looking to beat the averages and obtain results that cannot be found anywhere but in the United States.

After reading this book, you will have a plan that allows you to invest in real estate with a reasonable budget and to generate returns that far outweigh all other investment channels that you've previously considered.

You'll learn about investing in properties that are rented to tenants as part of the US Department of Housing and Urban Development (HUD) program known as Section 8. The Section 8 program involves renting (typically) lower-end houses and apartments to government-backed tenants. Through this program, local municipalities have been handed millions of dollars by the US government to pay lessors (landlords or landladies) who wish to accept tenants who require assistance to pay for their housing.

If you live in the United States, you might be within a few miles of existing investment properties that could provide you with these higher returns; you might drive by hundreds of these houses and apartments every day without realizing it because many of them are located in typical residential neighborhoods and look like any other home.

If you're looking to invest in real estate in the United States, Section 8 housing is very much within your means. Ownership is not limited to million-dollar funds, big financial institutions, or government agencies; it's available to anyone. For as little as $30,000, even an "Average Joe" can have a real estate investment with extraordinary returns. It really is a well-kept American secret.

This book isn't about teaching you the ins and outs of running to the courthouse steps and spending hours in auctions trying to pick up foreclosures. The goal of this book is to give you a clear understanding of the Section 8 program: what kind of real estate you should be buying, tips for navigating the system, some of the ins and outs of working with Section 8 tenants, and financial aspects of this type of investment. This book will also focus primarily on dealing with houses; the Section 8 program also deals with apartments, but those are beyond the scope of this book.

While the properties are in the United States, investors from all over the world have access to this unique investment. Even if you live thousands of miles away from the United States, this book will show you how simple it is to acquire this investment and have it operate efficiently without you having to spend more than five minutes a month checking on your property's performance.

CHAPTER 1

THE LANDSCAPE

In November 2009, the bank foreclosed on two Florida properties that I had bought at the height of the market in 2006. What a horrible feeling that was—all the money, energy, and emotions that were put into these properties were all gone, along with my credit score. The properties ended up selling for less than a third of the price I paid for them; clearly, I had myself to blame. Surely, I thought, it wasn't entirely the bank's fault.

But hundreds of thousands of people were faced with the same situation, and we all basically fell for it—the mind-set that the market was invincible. We were not calculating when it came to our investments; we were just following the crowds and imagining our wealth growing in front of our eyes.

The three years between the purchase of those two properties and their inevitable foreclosures was a period in which real estate became something I despised. It was, in essence, a complete joke that made my life miserable.

Let me explain: My first house cost $320,000, and the appraisal at the time came in at $320,000, so at least I was paying what it was worth, right? It was an amazing feeling, having come to this country at the age of fifteen from France and now living the true American dream of homeownership. In the booming market of the time, I envisioned making that property into a successful investment and making my parents proud. The property needed refurbishing, but I just knew that I would get back every penny I put into that house. The market was in a dizzying upward cycle, and I just *knew* that this was money well spent.

Soon the house reappraised for $360,000, and I was on my way to rehabbing it with a second mortgage. Everything was working out perfectly. My checkbook was on my hip all day, and money kept pouring out into this never-ending project, but it was okay, I thought. The house needed a new kitchen, new bathrooms, new floors, and new appliances, but I was sure that I would be able to recoup my costs in rental income while the market kept appreciating and that ultimately someone would buy the house for even more money than I had spent on it.

Then the US housing market crashed overnight. At the same time, my personal life had taken a turn, and I was forced to rent the property out. After going through three tenants in eighteen months and barely getting $1,600 per month in rent, I simply gave up on this property as a rental. All the problems with finding a tenant for the house—dealing with payment plans (instead of one-time payments), tenants calling for repairs and then not paying rent, neighbors calling to complain about late-night parties, evicting tenants, and changing locks—proved to be too much. How could it be so hard to fill a house with normal tenants in what was supposed to be a great neighborhood?

Even if I had the perfect tenant, the numbers didn't add up: $1,600 per month in rent for twelve months was $19,200. After $5,500 for property taxes, I was left with $13,700. On top of that, my mortgage payment was $1,700 per month, which added up to over $20,000 a year, so I was under by almost $7,000 due to all my expenses. So right there, even with a perfect tenant, I had to reach into my pocket to keep this home, creating a loss of income or a negative return on investment. That is called an *opportunity cost*, which is a cost that keeps you from investing in other ventures or assets that could actually make you money. Even if I didn't have a mortgage, the net return on my investment would be about 3.8 percent before taxes—essentially only one vacant month or major plumbing issue away from a zero return on investment.

Meanwhile, my other investment was a small condominium in Orlando—four hours away from Fort Lauderdale, where I resided at the time. That property was in a homeowner's association that was not giving parking permits to tenants, which ultimately meant that no one could rent my unit—yet I was still responsible for the association's $250 monthly fee.

The Orlando property ended up being auctioned off for $33,000, compared to my $158,000 purchase price. I can't tell you how bad it made me feel to lose that property in that manner, but I knew that I was accountable for my own actions. I had not done any calculations; I lived four hours from the property, I didn't use a management company, and I hadn't considered the impact the homeowner's association's decisions could have on my ability to rent the property.

Luckily, each crisis leads to an opportunity. At the time, I was working for Bank of America, and its employees were being asked to sell home equity lines of credit to everyone who entered the bank. The goal was to mortgage customers' homes that had increased in value and hand them massive amounts of money to play with based on the equity they supposedly had. We were basically handing out lines of credits against people's homes like we were ATM machines.

I saw clients take that home equity line of credit and invest it in products that depreciate in value, like a vehicle or a boat. Others would take those funds and purchase another overpriced property that was on the verge of losing all its value. On the flip side, one of my clients, who became a mentor and one of my closest friends, asked me to finance cheap properties in central Florida and Tampa with mortgages of about $50,000 to $75,000. Curious to understand what he was up to, we decided to fly to Tampa to gain more insight into the venture because he had done the math, and the numbers showed a clear and favorable return on investment. Even though real estate had been such a negative experience in my life, I wanted to see if you could truly enter a real estate environment that had the ability to offset your expenses and leave you with money in the bank when it's all said and done.

After landing at the Tampa airport, we joined my client's business partner in a drive through the streets of Tampa. Our goal was to view at least twenty-five homes before our flight back to Fort Lauderdale a few hours later.

I'll never forget that day: my client's business partner spent the entire six hours of our tour on the phone, negotiating with bank asset managers on different properties. It was quite eye-opening: asset managers for the banks were controlling everything, and with the goal of getting these houses off their banks' balance sheets, my client was a perfect customer.

Meanwhile, we were entering distressed homes, some of which were in such disrepair that I didn't even want to step through the front door. Sometimes there would be three such houses on the same street; it really felt like a Monopoly game, except it wasn't Boardwalk or Park Place that my client was buying.

In those houses I did enter, I tiptoed around wondering what I was going to discover in these smelly, gloomy, abandoned properties. My client, who wore white socks and khaki shorts, would come out of these houses covered with fleas; but while he stomped his way back to the car in an effort to dislodge the pests, he'd comment, "Wow, what a great house! Next!"

It was shocking to me. These houses had been abandoned, and entire streets were vacant; some areas looked like war zones. Copper pipes were stripped out, entire air conditioning units were stolen, roofs were caved in, kitchen appliances were missing, electric meters were gone, windows were boarded up.

But the reason my client was so excited was that he had figured out a way to get these bank-owned properties back in shape and then rent them to provide a very high return on investment. He was and still is a true entrepreneur, taking a nonperforming product and turning it around to get the most out of a real estate investment.

Seeing that many people across the country were getting involved in turning around properties that were part of the financial crisis, I thought, why couldn't I do the same in Fort Lauderdale, where I lived? Why couldn't I also assist investors in this opportunity of a lifetime?

In some areas during the tour with my client, we were looking at $50,000 to $80,000 homes that would rent for $900 to $1,200 per month and experience 15 percent net returns after renovations, taxes, and expenses. This gave me a new perspective on my $360,000 property that I had barely been able to rent for $1,600 and received a maximum of 3.8 percent net return. I realized there were solutions in real estate.

During the peak years of the housing crisis—2008 to 2010— thousands of homes were foreclosed on, and it was just a matter of having some cash and some key contacts within the banks for investors to get their hands on them. Banks had thousands of listings to look at and make offers on—the challenge was beating everyone to the line to get them. If you were an investor, you were looking at these homes as potential financial products that would bring in rental income and allow the investment to perform. Finally, investors had access to some solid products to invest in, and they were able to make decisions that made sense to them and were based on rental income and numbers.

As far as my clients were concerned, investing in distressed properties was a no-brainer as long as there was a partner involved in making these returns come to fruition: the property manager (in this case, me) who was charged with overseeing every property. Almost every day, clients asked me for lists of foreclosed properties. America was on sale, and people were looking to pick up thousands of properties like the ones that I had given back to the bank. The economy has since bounced back tremendously, but there are still thousands of properties up for grabs with the potential to provide you with significant returns.

In the early days, I operated my property management company, Ameristar Groupe, out of my car; I spent hours in my car and on my cell phone being the central phone number for everything from locating houses for sale to collecting rent from tenants to answering investor calls and e-mails. My glove box was filled with collected rent that I would deposit in my clients' accounts every month. The success of my clients' investments fell entirely on my shoulders, and it changed my entire outlook on life; I knew that their success and quality of life depended on my ability to make good decisions and to be available to them at all times.

Today, Ameristar Groupe employs a large number of people for the management of over a thousand properties. But we're not stopping there. Our goal is to offer products in different areas of the country for years to come and to make investors aware that these products exist while also preventing them from making other real estate investment mistakes.

As a native of France, offering these opportunities to European investors—helping them experience the American dream—seemed like the best fit for many of my company's early years, especially when the euro was comparatively strong. Then I realized that we could help anyone in the United States, and nearly any country, take advantage of these investment opportunities simply because, dollar for dollar, the return on investment was very strong. I travelled the world—Senegal, Thailand, France, India, Germany, and Morocco—to display these affordable homes, always with the message that I would be managing the investors' assets. That has been the key to our company's success—helping everyday investors get income from real estate with very little effort.

The key to return on investment in real estate is good management of the income that is produced by the product. Without the aid of a good management company, proper management requires a lot of hands-on time and resources from investors. For starters, it involves handling the rental of the property itself, which means dealing with tenants. You need to advertise the property, communicate with potential tenants, physically show up at the property to get a signature on a lease, hand over the keys, and more.

You must also collect rent and calculate into the investment equation the chance that a tenant will leave before the end of a lease, forcing you to quickly find a new tenant to provide the rental income. In addition to the departure of a tenant, you may also be forced to deal with repairs and fluctuations in property taxes, interest rates, insurance costs, and other factors beyond your control. If the property you're renting out brings in $1,300 a month in rent but costs you more than that in upkeep, then it's up to you to make up the difference. If you're counting on that rental income for your own living expenses, then your asset is quickly going to become a liability.

JUST WHAT IS HUD SECTION 8?

Created in 1937 during the Great Depression to alleviate the housing crisis of the time, the HUD Section 8 program remains in existence and is regularly updated. Because there are consistently people in the United States who require support to pay for shelter, there continues to be a very large budget for housing assistance. In fact, more than $20 billion is currently dedicated to tenant-based rental assistance subsidies.[1]

For investors, Section 8 housing offers more than just a monthly paycheck—it's also a way of helping out families in need. Often, we work with panicked tenants who have only two weeks to find a place to live, but we find them a house because we happen to have the product. That feels good.

Across the country, there are hundreds of thousands of families who make less than 50 percent of the median national household income, which qualifies them for housing subsidies through the HUD Section 8 program. Regardless of their financial situation, people need a safe place to live and raise their families. They want to live in a decent home in a decent neighborhood, but for any number of reasons they can't live in a middle-class neighborhood or in a rural area. Many factors contribute to how likely a person or family is to successfully lease a unit qualifying for the voucher program. Some factors include: "the characteristics of the voucher holder's household; the motivation

---

1 "Section 8 Voucher Funding and Reform," National Alliance to End Homelessness, accessed October 4, 2015, http://www.endhomelessness.org/pages/section_8.

and search effort of the voucher holder; factors affecting desirability as a tenant (e.g., credit history); the voucher holder's understanding of program rules; PHA policies and procedures; pre-program living conditions; the tightness of the housing market; and the degree to which local landlords accept Section 8.[2]

Success Rates by Demographic Characteristics

	Percent of all Households	Success Rate
Race Ethnicity		
White non-Hispanic	19%	69%
Black non-Hispanic	*56%*	*68%*
Hispanic	22%	68%
Other	2%	73%
Age of Head of Household		
Less than 25	18%	73%
25 to 44	*59%*	*68%*
45 to 61	17%	70%
62 or Older	7%	54%
Gender of Head of Household		
Female	*83%*	*69%*
Male	17%	64%
Household Size/Disability		
1 person not elderly, not disabled	8%	56%
1 person elderly, not disabled	1%	63%
1 person elderly and disabled	3%	54%
1 person not elderly but disabled	9%	74%
2 people	24%	69%
3-4 people	*41%*	*72%*
5+ people	14%	67%
Household Composition		
Not elderly, with Children	*74%*	*70%*
Elderly	7%	54%
Disabled, single	10%	73%
Not elderly or disabled, no children	9%	56%
Preference Homeless		
Yes	*6%*	*60%*
No	94%	69%
Income Relative to Local Median		
Income = $0	4%	63%
$0<Income <=30% of Local Median	*75%*	*71%*
Income > 30% of Local Median	21%	59%

2 U.S. Department of Housing and Urban Development Office of Policy Development and Research, "Study on Section 8 Voucher Success Rates: Volume 1 Quantitative Study of Success Rates in Metropolitan Areas," November 2001.

Many Section 8 tenants are single mothers who have very few options for housing in neighborhoods where they can raise their children under normal, safe conditions. For example, a woman in southern Florida making less than $25,000 a year and trying to raise three children will have trouble finding suitable housing in a safe neighborhood without government assistance. According to the Economic Policy Institute's Family Budget Calculator, as of the writing of this book, one parent with three children would need to make more than $80,000 annually to afford to live in the Fort Lauderdale area.[3]

As part of the HUD Section 8 program, the government allows investors to not only own the homes that lower-income renters live in but to also collect a subsidy for making those homes acceptable places to live.

The voucher piece of the Section 8 program was initiated in 1983. Housing vouchers are available to any qualified individual and are used to pay rent while the recipients are tenants in any qualified property.

Housing choice vouchers are administered locally by public housing agencies (PHAs), which receive federal funds from HUD to administer the voucher program. Families are issued housing vouchers to help pay for suitable housing; houses rented to Section 8 tenants must meet minimum standards of health and safety, as determined by the PHA.[4] Each voucher beneficiary is allowed to choose his or her lodgings, and the voucher's value is calculated according to rental market prices in the tenant's area.

The list below shows the rates at which people of varying demographics successfully lease a unit qualifying for the Housing Choice Voucher (HCV) program.

---

3 "Family Budget Calculator," Economic Policy Institute, accessed August 24, 2015, http://www.epi.org/resources/budget/.
4 "Housing Choice Vouchers Fact Sheet," US Department of Housing and Urban Development, accessed August 24, 2015, http://portal.hud.gov/hudportal/HUD?src=/topics/housing_choice_voucher_program_section_8.

A housing subsidy is paid to the lessor directly by the PHA to assist in the rent paid for the property on behalf of the tenant. The tenant pays any difference between the actual rent charged by the lessor and the amount subsidized by the program. The PHA calculates the maximum amount of housing assistance allowable, and under some circumstances, if authorized by the PHA, a family may use its voucher to purchase a modest home.[5]

This flowchart shows how housing choice vouchers for Section 8 housing are funded, administered, and redeemed.

The HCV Relationships

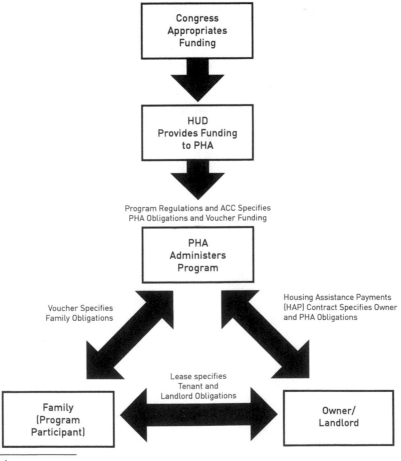

5 Ibid.

When a Section 8 family selects a home and it is approved by the PHA, the family signs a minimum one-year lease with the lessor. After one year and after an annual inspection, the lease is renewed for another twelve months. Once in the home, the family is expected to comply with the requirements of the lease and the program, which include paying rent on time, maintaining the condition of the property, and notifying the PHA of changes in income or family makeup.[6]

Lessors in the HUD Section 8 program must also meet certain standards to remain in the Section 8. These include providing safe and sanitary housing at a reasonable rent and providing services agreed to in the lease.[7]

---

6 Ibid.
7 Ibid.

The figure below shows how households participate in the Section 8 program.

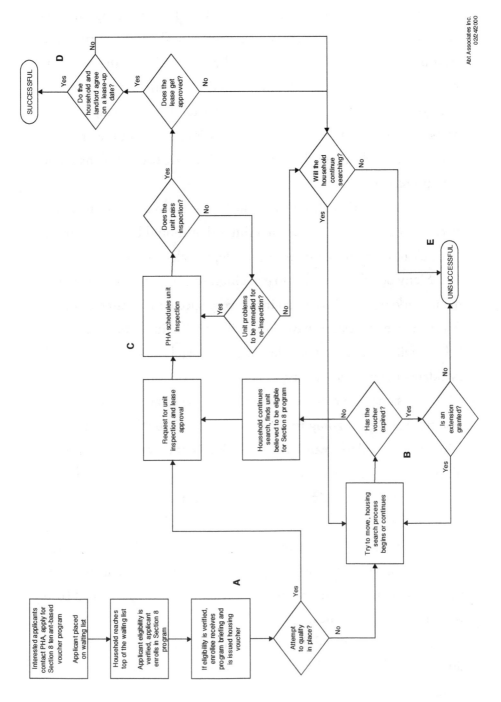

THE EMOTIONAL INVESTOR

Since discovering the HUD Section 8 housing program, my life has been spent helping investors find affordable properties and creating income streams to improve their lives. Along the way, one key aspect that has had to be monitored is the investors' emotions. The goal has been to get people to understand that buying a rental property is not about what color the house is or how nice the driveway looks but is solely about the numbers and having backup plans B and C to protect their money.

As I've mentioned, investing in Section 8 real estate is a very attractive option, but it's not something that should be done without some clear, up-front planning and in-depth calculations.

Many people think that to get a high return in traditional investment markets, they have to go into a very speculative frame of mind. For instance, investors have lost millions buying stock that they believe will double or land that will ultimately host the next Jack Nicklaus-designed golf course.

That same frame of mind happens in real estate. Many investors assume that they're going to buy a house for $200,000 and sell it for $300,000; they don't realize that those kinds of deals are uncommon. Television shows depict investors flipping a house in two months for twice the initial price, but those are people who've been in the business for years, and the episodes don't show the battles lost—they only highlight the wins. Numerous times, I have talked with intelligent people who are still paying for real estate investment mistakes they made years ago; they're stuck covering fees and operational costs that are in the thousands.

To take unpredictability and speculation out of the picture, we don't particularly consider what a house is worth and what it may sell for down the road. Instead, we consider what it can be rented for. If you pay $100,000 for a house, rent it for $1,300 a month, and keep it for ten years, you're going to get your money back through the rental income. Show me a product where you can make your money back in ten years with a price point starting at $100,000. Products like this do exist in cities like Fort Lauderdale, Baltimore, Detroit, Atlanta, and Memphis, some of the areas hardest hit by the housing crisis.

Geographic Patterns of Above Average Success Rates

	Public Housing Agency	Success Rate
1	Akron	58
2	Alameda	37
3	Albuquerque	100
4	Allegheny County	55
5	Atlanta	60
6	Baltimore County	57
7	Boston	53
8	Bridgeport	47
9	Chicago	82
10	Cook County	68
11	Corpus Christi	67
12	Cuyahoga	88
13	Dallas	66
14	Dayton Metro	60
15	Des Moines	66
16	**DETROIT**	**100**
17	El Paso	96
18	Everett	88
19	Grand Prairie	78
20	Hartford	89
21	Indianapolis	76
22	Kenosha	84
23	Lexington-Fayette County	63
24	Los Angeles City	47
25	Los Angeles County	77
26	Metro Council Minn/St Paul	62
27	Miami-Dade County	71
28	Milwaukee County	69
29	Monmouth-Ocean Counties	93
30	Montgomery County	42
31	New Orleans	68
32	New York City	56
33	Newark	100
34	Newport News	69
35	Oklahoma City	57
36	Phoenix	82
37	Pinellas County	38
38	Plymouth	68
39	Prince George's County	78
40	San Buenaventura	48
41	San Diego	88
42	St. Louis County	52
43	Syracuse	97
44	Tucson	72
45	Tulsa	69
46	Washington, DC	58

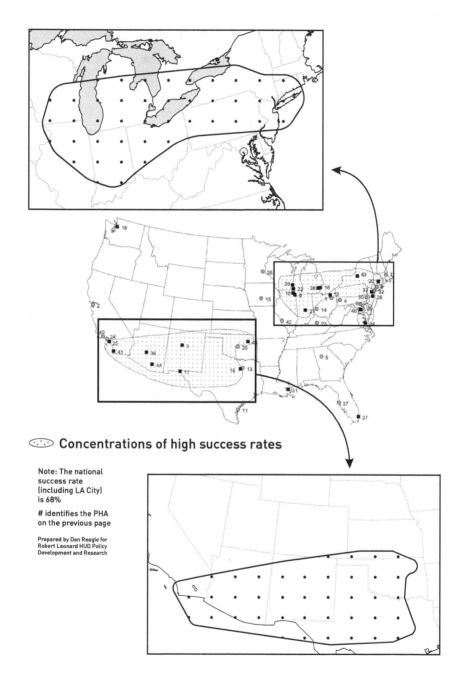

⬭⬭⬭ **Concentrations of high success rates**

Note: The national
success rate
(including LA City)
is 68%

identifies the PHA
on the previous page

Prepared by Dan Reagle for
Robert Leonard HUD Policy
Development and Research

And investors in this type of housing are abundant; there are a lot more people in the world with $50,000 or $100,000 in the bank then there are with $5,000,000. Some people have savings that they want to invest in real estate—whether in a cash deal or through some sort of leverage with the bank—but they don't know what realistic options are available to them. The vast majority of people who want to invest in real estate fall into a funnel of basic options that they've been familiar with for years, usually because of the experience of a family member or friend. Buy a rental property in an urban area, a university town, or some sunny location, and then just sit back and collect a rent check every month. Easy, right?

When it comes to investing, what often happens is that emotions dominate the decision-making process. Within a year or two of making an investment, many investors realize that their ego got in the way of making a sound decision that provides a real return. Some people leave significant funds sitting in various accounts for years on end without receiving any real income, or their funds are in volatile investments that they ignore because they don't want to acknowledge the poor performance they're getting. At that point, it's just a matter of accepting defeat: sell, roll over into another product, or simply kiss the investment good-bye, like I was forced to do with real estate at the peak of the market.

How is your money performing for you right now? If you look at your current investment situation, would you agree that it's not as interesting as you would like it to be? Maybe your portfolio isn't even generating any real income, which was surely the original plan. So what happened? If your investments are in real estate, you may even be reaching into your pocket to maintain those assets, and those pockets tend to become emptier and emptier if you're in the wrong type of real estate. For instance, if you're a "fix-and-flipper," you're speculating on a big price inflation that will allow you to make a profit. Often, these predictions go wrong, and the result is a far cry from enjoying the benefits of a great flip.

As an investor, you want optimal performance from the product that you are acquiring with your hard-earned money, in real estate and elsewhere. You also want to conserve what you have, protect what you have achieved, and comfort yourself with the knowledge that you have made the right decisions. This is easier said than done; sometimes investors make bad decisions because they just don't have enough information up front—they don't think of all the important questions, or they're too timid to ask.

Each time you develop an interest in a specific investment channel, you need to find supporting facts and figures that give you confidence that what you're interested in is the best fit for you because once you transfer the funds to acquire that asset, you are all alone—forget the friend who recommended that you jump into that amazing stock, forget the business partner who told you about that great parcel of land that would appreciate, forget the uncle who told you to buy a building in a hot, up-and-coming market. In any of these scenarios, your best friend was the online banking screen with the "confirm transfer" button that gave you one last chance to recognize how stubborn or naive you were in following what someone told you to do.

But what if you could press that "confirm transfer" button and feel confident in the decision you made? Instead of anxiety, what if you could feel a sense of freedom? What if you felt that the button you just clicked was going to lead to the fulfillment of your needs, a long-awaited goal, or a new direction in life? Personally, I love hitting that button and then picturing that money on the computer screen transforming itself into brick and mortar—what an amazing rush!

And that's the kind of emotion you want when investing in entry-price real estate: the emotion of confidence that the money has been spent on a product that will provide sound economic figures and perform well for you.

As I mentioned earlier, I was one of those people caught up in the financial crisis of the mid-2000s, which resulted in millions of Americans having their property seized. In 2008 alone, there were 861,664 foreclosures and more than 3.1 million foreclosure filings issued.[8] By the end of 2014, the trend had dramatically improved, but RealtyTrac—a comprehensive housing data resource—still reported 1.1 million properties with foreclosure filings in 2014.[9]

The consequences of the American financial crisis have been twofold: first, banks, keen to get rid of these assets, have been selling them off at low prices; second, there has been a very high demand for rental property due to the growing population and former home-owners now obliged to rent.

In Florida, the impact has been especially dramatic. In 2007, house prices plummeted to half or even one-third of their value, depending on location. When housing valuations dropped, the properties were abandoned by their owners and became distressed. Today, houses that were purchased for $180,000 to $250,000 are regularly being sold for $75,000 to $80,000. Many of these houses are ideal for the HUD Section 8 program.

It's interesting to note that real estate values did not become depressed in other parts of the world. Europe's real estate values have maintained themselves over the last several decades and have even

8 "Foreclosures Up a Record 81% in 2008," CNN Money, accessed February 9, 2016, http://money.cnn.com/2009/01/15/real_estate/millions_in_foreclosure/.

9 1.1 Million U.S. Properties with Foreclosure Filings in 2014, Down 18 Percent from 2013 to Lowest Level Since 2006," RealityTrac Newsroom and Media Center," January 15, 2015, accessed February 9, 2016, http://www.realtytrac.com/news/foreclosure-trends/1-1-million-u-s-properties-with-foreclosure-filings-in-2014-down-18-percent-from-2013-to-lowest-level-since-2006/.

gone up in value (albeit in a very minimal way). Conversely, when banks in the United States began lending to borrowers with lower credit ratings, those borrowers began defaulting when interest rates rose and economic growth slowed, and as a result, housing prices plummeted. Consequently, many investors tried to take advantage of the opportunity, but without any real understanding of the situation, they fell back on what they knew: traditional real estate investments that provided very little in the way of return. So as quickly as investors jumped into a crisis that they sought to take advantage of, they're now looking to exit those investments after what they consider to be a disappointing result or a nonperforming asset.

In most cities in the United States, there are distressed or depreciated houses that have significantly deflated values, and these properties are a very viable way for investors to take advantage of the real estate landscape as it is today. However, don't be fooled by price. You may think that you can purchase a house for significantly less than it's worth, but remember that the prices of homes were artificially inflated by the banking system; they were never worth what people paid for them. Instead, what you're paying for distressed houses today is pretty much what they're worth until you fix them up and stabilize them for rental income.

CHAPTER 1 TAKEAWAYS

- The US housing crisis has resulted in new entry-level real estate opportunities for investors.
- Buying a rental property is not about the color of the house or how nice the driveway is; it's about property's ability to make you money.
- For investors, Section 8 housing is an excellent opportunity to make your money perform for you while also helping families in need find safe, affordable housing.
- Investing in distressed properties is a no-brainer, as long as you have a property manager making sure the returns come to fruition for you.
- Ameristar Groupe specializes in helping people all over the world take advantage of affordable, high-yield real estate investment opportunities.

CHAPTER 2

THINK BEFORE YOU CLICK

Miscalculations are the cause of many business failures, and it's no different with real estate—if you don't do the math at the onset of the venture, then you could end up losing your shirt. That's why it's best to look at real estate investments from a financial—rather than emotional—point of view.

A real estate investment—whether it is a $50,000 investment or a million-dollar investment—requires analysis and very solid numbers up front. If your logic is that as long as the rent covers the mortgage you're fine, that means you're in a speculative investment where you anticipate the prices to rise and that you'll make a profit when its time to sell. That doesn't take into consideration other factors that could be financially detrimental in the long run. You may be unable to find tenants for some of your investments, and some investments will require constant upkeep on top of your property taxes to be paid. If an investment is not performing as well as you thought or can't be developed due to a third-party failing, it can bring stress and financial difficulties into your life.

My message throughout this book solely relates to the residential real estate market. I believe that thousands of people aspire to be part of this market just to fulfill a feeling of owning, growing, and dominating what I view as a life-sized Monopoly game board.

As a residential investor, it feels great to tell your friends that you just closed on a property. This is especially true if you live in another country and you just closed on your first US home; you'll want to tell the whole neighborhood that you own a piece of American soil. That moment is a chance to really be proud and to demonstrate to others that you have the courage and motivation to reach outside your comfort zone and do what many others would never risk.

What I'm talking about is a different business model. Regardless of what country you live in, there are specific steps to access certain properties in the United States that provide living space for families while providing you with higher returns. But you need to develop the know-how to access those products, and then you need the property managers to place families in those high-performing properties.

Just as every crisis opens up an opportunity, the housing crash was clearly a situation that we're still able to benefit from. Toxic loans led to thousands of abandoned properties that are now depreciated yet still saleable real estate. Depreciated real estate allows you to have higher return on investment based on the mere fact that market rents do not depend on the price of the house. For example, a three-bedroom, two-bath house in a certain neighborhood will rent for the same price regardless of if it just lost 100,000 in value.

The work my company does takes the emotion out of the equation and performs all the calculations before buying decisions are made.

WHY SECTION 8 HOUSING?

I started my company providing housing to families who didn't require any financial assistance. The vast majority of the houses that I invested in and managed were rented for about $1,300 a month. Then, around Christmas in 2010, I realized that, of the fifty or so homes that I was managing, not a single rent had been paid by families who were supposedly able to afford that $1,300 rent. That was a big turning point because I realized that, in order to collect rent that month, we were going to have to drop the rents down to $1,200 or $1,000, but that meant sacrificing the return on investment. Since neither I nor my investors had the means to offer free housing, I decided that it was time to research the world of Section 8.

Up until that time, I thought Section 8 was an exclusive investment channel only available to big investment firms, but I quickly found out that anyone who owned a rental property could be part of the Section 8 program. Section 8, I decided, would hedge against the issue of traditional tenants who ran into financial difficulties and avoided paying rent altogether.

I began by building relationships with government agencies; meeting with social workers; and learning to deal with additional paperwork, requirements, inspections, etc. This was a major turning point; once we had the program up and running, rent payments were coming in from the government on the third of every month, and the amounts were larger than those submitted by my traditional tenants.

The $1,300 that I was having trouble collecting from traditional tenants had turned into a steady $1,400 or $1,500.

Once I turned to Section 8, my investors became more confident, and all I had to do was explain how the program worked and how it could help them reach their income goals. Later in the book, I'll go into detail about the various questions and fears that investors had about Section 8, but let me briefly give the answers to a few of the more common ones: tenants in the Section 8 program rely on vouchers to help them pay their rent; there are thousands of properties waiting to be qualified as Section 8; there's a higher supply of tenants than there are houses; and as a government-backed program, there are many measures in place to protect both lessors (investors) and tenants.

THREE MUST-HAVES BEFORE INVESTING

Before entering into any kind of investment, there are three things you must have: the motivation, the means, and a sense of trust.

Whether you live in the United States or overseas, you must first have the motivation to invest in real estate. This sounds obvious, but many people never develop the desire to invest in anything. For example, maybe you love chocolate, but you don't necessarily want to invest in forestland in Costa Rica where cacao is grown. Or maybe you love Florida, but you only want to spend vacation time there rather than investing in rental real estate.

So Section 8 investment begins with wanting to invest in a specific product that is the fulfillment of a long-time dream or ambition. or simply because you want to manage the risk of your investment with the security of government-subsidized income.

Once you are certain that real estate is the type of investment you're after, the second thing you must have is the means to make such an investment, or you must take steps to generate savings or get financing to allow you to make that purchase. Without the means, all you can do is sit on the sidelines, listening and watching as others invest.

Now, investors sometimes go to extraordinary lengths to take advantage of an investment or to enter into a new venture; they may scrape together their own money, ask for help from friends and family, borrow from hard money lenders, or sacrifice existing, stable assets. Often, in these instances, the ego is the driving force— investors jumping through too many hoops to make an investment in real estate may be better off recognizing that they are being held hostage by their emotions. It may be better to accept the fact that this may not be the right time to make such an investment—your life will not fall apart if you miss one opportunity.

In fact, sometimes investors find themselves happier for not having made an investment in real estate after hearing horror stories of people who have lost everything. Those were people who had the desire and the means, but they were missing a key third requirement—trust.

Developing trust is a real estate agent's biggest nightmare, but it is the investor's biggest safety net; as the investor, you must have a level of trust in the salesperson who's presenting you the product, whether it's a forest in Costa Rica, solar panel projects in northern Africa, or a house in California.

In every real estate investment, you are going to have to trust someone in order to move forward into a transaction. For example, imagine that you love a property and have the means to purchase it, but you don't trust the agent who is selling the house to you. That discomfort you feel could easily turn into the discovery that something is amiss right after you send the money for the transaction.

As the investor, you must also feel that same sense of trust for any property manager you hire to oversee your house. If you don't trust something about a property manager's operations, then you're probably better off walking away. If you go against your intuition and purchase the property to manage yourself, then you must trust that you have the capability and the know-how to do so. You will also have to trust that you have made the proper calculations and that your goals will be met. Investing in a Section 8 property requires trust on several levels: trust that the system will be around for years to come, trust that the tenants placed in your property will be reliable, and trust that the management company involved has the means to oversee the constant requirements to maintain your qualification as a Section 8 landlord.

Without these components in place—the motivation, the means, and a sense of trust—you will likely feel that your money is being thrown into an empty hole that will create an immediate loss or will never produce any return on your investment. Most of the time, if you're missing one of the three must-haves, you simply never advance toward making that investment, and the years go by without having committed to anything.

REAL ESTATE FROM YOUR COUCH

Investors want to get paid as quickly as possible once they have pressed the "confirm transfer" button, or as I also like to call it, the "investment button." Soon after turning to Section 8 housing, I realized that it was a lot easier to assist investors in their quest to be lessors by providing them with a finished product that already had a tenant. This provided them with *cash flow from day one.*

What that meant for me was doing all the hard work on the front end to renovate and stabilize the house, or the *product*, as we call it. Basically, my company is the initial investor, and then we provide an income platform that benefits a new investor from the day he or she purchases the property. It sounds simple, but you won't find a lot of opportunities around the country that provide this all-in-one service.

My solution allows you to fulfill a dream, whatever the size of your wallet. Our clientele is very diverse—young couples who have saved a bit of money over time, retirees, professionals who have sold their business, experienced investors, and people who have received an inheritance or have early career earnings; in short, people who are eager to find a solution for their idle money and who are looking to build a nice portfolio.

The bottom line is that people who wish to invest in cheap rental homes come from all over the world. Regardless of their financial backgrounds, there is one common problem that we are able to solve for them: generating returns from a company-managed, turnkey income property.

It gets even easier when you see how practical the American system is when it comes to actually buying a property. Most people assume you will need to physically go to the region where your investment property is and sign documents on-site. In reality, the entire transaction can actually take place via e-mail and overnight delivery. Many countries require the equivalent of a phonebook of paperwork to acquire a property. You might think that, as law driven and procedural as America is, the process would be similar here, but America has it down to a fairly minimal amount of paperwork. It's actually quite common to find title companies with offices several hundred miles away from a subject property that are capable of completing the entire transaction between the seller and buyer.

For some investors, it's impossible to go through a process of buying a property without seeing it. But more than 70 percent of our clients haven't seen their property before they purchase it. With the Internet and Google Street View, it's fairly simple to wander through streets and neighborhoods around the world. This is an ideal way to grasp the look and feel of an area and to get a sense of comfort that your investment dollars are being spent in neighborhoods that are usually well maintained and reasonable places for low-income families to live. You can sit in your living room in Singapore and "drive" through the streets of Miami or Detroit, looking at investment properties.

Once you have made the decision to buy a property, you are also able to use today's technologies to acquire the asset without leaving your home. Then, with a few months of rent in your bank account, you can use that money to travel to the property and make both a business and leisure trip of it. Most of our clients are able to plan a trip to see their investment properties at a time that is convenient for their work and family schedules.

CHAPTER 2 TAKEAWAYS

- Smart real estate investments require analysis of solid numbers up front.
- Anyone who owns a rental property can be a part of Section 8 housing.
- Section 8 housing offers property owners protection because the government guarantees a percentage of the rent.
- The three things real estate investors must have are:
    1. The motivation to invest in real estate

    2. The means to invest

    3. Trust in Section 8 and your property manager

- The American real estate system makes buying and managing property easy, even from outside the US.

CHAPTER 3

THE INCOME TRIFECTA

As you can imagine, it can be a challenge to locate homes worthy of rehabilitation, but ideal properties do exist. The key is to look for properties where the numbers make sense: properties that, once rehabbed with a normal (not extravagant) budget, will bring in a rental income that provides a good return on investment.

So which is a better investment: the big house in the nice neighborhood, or the small house in a neighborhood that you would not dare to live in? It really depends on what you're looking for, but this is where your business mind has to kick in to remove emotions from the equation. When looking at housing to purchase to place Section 8 tenants in, it's not about finding a place for you to live in. It's about finding a house in a neighborhood nice enough for a family to live in and rent from you for the long term with the support of the government.

Nobody—from the billionaires of the world to the high school kid mowing lawns on weekend—wants to lose money. Houses that qualify for Section 8 tenants allow you to make the highest income possible with the smallest investment. It's human nature to want to make the most money with the smallest commitment. But you really need to look at this as a balanced investment that provides you with what I call the "Income Trifecta": security, income, and liquidity.

What that means is that the small house in the bad neighborhood is probably not your best investment, but neither is the big house in the middle- to upper-class neighborhood.

SECURITY

The first piece of the Income Trifecta is *security*. When looking at potential investment houses, you want to examine the security of the area both for the product itself and for your future tenant. In the United States, you can invest in properties for as little as $5,000— sometimes even less. But depending on the area, these lowest-priced products are not always the best deal for your dollar. Often, these are in neighborhoods that are frightening even in the middle of the day, much less at night. Why would a tenant want to live in an area that poses so many security risks? Moreover, the costs involved in turning that property around to make it a performing asset could be $30,000, totaling $35,000, and now you run the risk of having a property costing you more than its worth. That can be okay if the rents are providing an excellent return on investment, taking the emotions out of what the property is worth today and in the future, and allowing you to produce a return far better than any local bank will provide you.

When working on properties in unsafe areas, it can be discouraging to go into a property and find that it's been stripped by burglars of all copper pipes and electrical wiring. When thieves remove $40 or

$100 worth of electrical wires, they typically create $800 to $1,000 in labor costs from the damage they do when ripping the components out of the walls.

There are a few points in time when the security of the product is critical. The first is at the beginning of any acquisition—if you have missing copper pipes, you will most likely need a plumbing permit to get those reinstalled. That's okay—it's sometimes expected—but if your house is in a bad area, how are you going to keep the newly installed pipes from also being stolen before you get a family moved in?

Another point in time when you need to be especially concerned about the security of your property is when a tenant is moving out. In many areas, this is when your property becomes a target; people familiar with the activity at the house may realize that no one is living there and break in to snatch whatever they can get, including appliances, copper pipes, electrical wires, and the air conditioner. This is why, in certain neighborhoods that are not optimal, it's recommended that you don't put a "for rent" sign on the front yard. What that sign really says is "vacant house, please take everything that's inside."

We have a contingency plan in place. We actually hire people to sleep in our houses to protect the property; they are hired to occupy the property during the period of transition between one tenant moving out and another tenant moving in. But as much as possible, you want to avoid getting into properties in areas where there are concerns that thieves may remove your renovation upgrades as soon as they are installed.

Take it from someone who has experienced this frustration. We had one house where we had to install three electrical panels while we were trying to get the tenant in. Literally, the panel was stolen twice while we were renovating. You have to learn from these frustrating experiences and understand how to avoid them down the road. Now we have welders who install cages or grills around the electric meter and the air conditioning unit so that they can't be stolen.

If you get into properties that are in very low-income areas, you expose yourself to increased risk of theft and break-ins, which obviously are a hindrance to your income and your profit-and-loss statements. Instead of a worthwhile investment, you have a property that is basically a source of loot for burglars. It takes a special investor to accept those kinds of conditions and to put in systems that protect your property. It's not impossible to work with these kinds of properties and to get tenants to live there, but once you manage to get a tenant in, you really need to work at keeping that tenant for years. This is a key message that I'll repeat throughout this book.

Section 8 tenants statistically have at least one child, and therefore your house is best when near a school and in a low crime area. Evidently, buying a cheap house and hoping for it to be in a safe neighborhood is a complicated task, but within poor neighborhoods, you can distinguish the bad from the really bad. Just ask the people living there; they won't hide from you if the area is a real issue. People who live in Section 8 housing want the same stability as people in traditional housing; many of them even see themselves owning a home someday. Just because they come from a less fortunate background and have few resources for getting by doesn't mean they don't have aspirations for the future.

This is a key consideration that connects your investment not only to an income strategy but also to an exit strategy. Think about it: someone who moves into your rental property might make an offer on your investment down the road, allowing you to profit from your investment after also benefiting from years of rental income. The security piece of the trifecta relies on you choosing a home that is a worthy investment for the long term.

INCOME

Now let's look at the *income* piece of the trifecta. Let's say that you've found and invested in a property, and while you're planting the "for rent" sign in the yard, someone passing by yells at you, wanting to know how much you're asking for rent. At that moment, you feel powerful; you're holding a piece of real estate that someone wants from you. Your emotions will kick in at the thought of already having found a potential tenant. You're not even thinking of why this person wants to rent the house from you. For all you know, they might have just been kicked out of a property or just committed domestic violence and need a place to stay in. And what about their income? Can they actually afford this house? Do they make three times the rent that you're asking? If you end up renting in this emotional state, you might find yourself chasing rent every month instead of getting a strong return on your investment. You may even be tempted to try to sell the property just to get out from under the mess you got yourself into, but who is going to buy a house that seems to always attract a troublesome tenant? Screening your tenants and identifying their ability to afford the rent is key to securing your own income.

This is an example of focusing too much on income and cheap pricing and losing sight of the need to balance income with the security and liquidity of your investment. For us the best way to ensure income is to make our properties Section 8 compliant. It allows us to make the property available to a tenant who is looking for a safe, comfortable place to live, and more often than not, you end up with higher rents backed by the government.

LIQUIDITY

The third piece of the trifecta is *liquidity*. It's important to remember that the best homes are those that are attractive when it comes time to resell—three/twos or four/twos (three- or four-bedroom houses with two bathrooms) are best. You may find yourself looking at houses that seem to be a good deal and that have two or six bedrooms, but again, if you want to hit that trifecta of security, income, and liquidity, then the midrange houses are the best. These houses tend to create better retention with renters as well.

Again, the goal is to provide your tenant with the most normal living conditions possible. This will give you steady income because the tenant will stay longer, and then you will have a product that will be an attractive sell to a future investor.

In Florida, where our headquarters are located, we've identified that most optimally performing properties start around $85,000 and go up to $135,000 in price. From there, we might have from $5,000 to $25,000 in repairs, depending on how good the roof is. If you look at housing with costs below these figures, you're standing on unstable ground; if you go above these figures, you're going to have diminishing returns—rents that don't follow a growth curve as strong as that provided by Section 8. This is the Income Trifecta "sweet spot," where products tend to be obtained for cheaper than face value.

In other areas of the country, you might have to spend a little more or a little less. For instance, Detroit can be a very affordable market where properties can be picked up for $25,000, but again, there is a strict selection process required to fall in the Income Trifecta "sweet spot." The criteria for buying Section 8 properties in a specific area are as follows:

1. Security: Find a home that is clearly in a livable area for a family with kids.
2. Income: Avoid going for the very inexpensive or the very high-end property.
3. Liquidity: Look for homes that have the ability to attract a buyer in the future.

By now I hope you're getting the message: there is no need to lose money in real estate. The key is to focus on properties that give you stability and consistent results, year in and year out. Section 8 housing is, for us, a program that provides that perfect combination.

Below you will see a chart that defines the payment standards by voucher bedroom size in Detroit and Fort Lauderdale.

Detroit Housing Commission Payment Standards by Voucher Bedroom Size, Effective December 11, 2015[10]

*The amounts shown are not guaranteed contract amounts

Voucher Bedroom Size	Payment Standard
0	$585
1	$724
2	$949
3	$1,263
4	$1,357
5	$1,561
6	$1,764

10 Rent Reasonableness & Payment Standards Effective December 11, 2015," Detroit Housing Commission, accessed February 23, 2016, http://www.dhcmi.org/pageind. aspx?page_id=1.

Fort Lauderdale FY 2015 Fair Market Rents for Existing Housing[11]

Bedroom Size	Fair Market Rent Standard
0	$764
1	$994
2	$1,263
3	$1,801
4	$2,237

Payment standards are used to calculate the housing assistance payment (HAP) that the PHA pays to the owner on behalf of the family leasing the unit. Each PHA has latitude in establishing its schedule of payment standard amounts by bedroom size. Some of these voucher amounts are significant—over $1,500 per month. $1,500 per month gives you $18,000 per year. If you have a $130,000 property, you could experience an almost 14 percent gross return ($18,000 divided by $130,000). That certainly is better than what your savings account at the bank is paying you, which is probably less than 1 percent per year.

The key is to identify what price you would have to pay for a house to rent it at $1,500 per month without the support of a government voucher. To get that same $1,500 per month rent outside the Section 8 program, you would probably have to spend $200,000, which would bring you less than 10 percent gross returns. That may still sound pretty good, but what I'm talking about is the Income Trifecta sweet spot. With the extra $100,000 you would spend on a traditional rental property, you could actually purchase another Section 8 property, leading to additional rental income of maybe

---

11 Final Fair Market Rents for the Housing Choice Voucher Program and Moderate Rehabilitation Single Room Occupancy Program Fiscal Year 2015," Department of Housing and Urban Development, " accessed February 23, 2016, https://www.novoco.com/hud/resource_files/fedreg/fedreg_100214.pdf.

$1,300 per month and a 14.6 percent overall return ($2,800 total rent per month yields $33,600 per year, divided by $230,000).

Below are examples of house prices and rents that I have positioned investors on who were looking for solid returns with the security of Section 8 to support a constant flow of income.

Price	Monthly Rent	Monthly Return on Investment	Annual Return on Investment
$85,000	$1,650	1.9%	23.3%
$76,000	$1,300	1.7%	20.5%
$68,000	$1,100	1.6%	19.4%
$64,000	$950	1.5%	17.8%
$52,000	$750	1.4%	17.3%
$106,000	$1,500	1.4%	17.0%
$88,000	$1,200	1.4%	16.4%
$122,000	$1,650	1.4%	16.2%
$97,000	$1,200	1.2%	14.8%
$91,000	$1,100	1.2%	14.5%
$118,000	$1,350	1.1%	13.7%
$114,000	$1,250	1.1%	13.2%
$104,000	$1,100	1.1%	12.7%
$95,000	$1,000	1.1%	12.6%

These investments are representative of what I consider to be the sweet spot in US real estate.

SOURCING PRODUCT

As an investor or real estate entrepreneur, the top issue you're confronted with is where to find Section 8 properties. You must continuously investigate different sourcing channels because for every twenty-five offers you make, you might get lucky to actually have a chance to purchase two houses. This is because inexpensive houses, or products, are accessible to far more people than expensive products.

Whichever channels you use, sourcing requires a lot of work and includes researching essentially any source of real estate information including advertisements, online sources, and preforeclosure public records. You must also reach out to asset managers, agents, and agencies, and you may even want to do mass mailings to locate properties.

You also need to have expertise with auctions, which is one way to acquire properties online. As with in-person auctions, you should do your research in advance of the actual sale by driving by and analyzing whether the property would make a good rental—again, by doing the calculations. An inspection in advance of the sale can also let you know what price point you're willing to entertain.

In addition, you'll need to build very strong relationships with bank brokers who deal in what are known as *real estate owned* (REO) properties, foreclosures that have been taken back by the lender who hasn't been able to sell it. One issue with REO properties is that banks tend to sell them to people who will live in the property; banks often don't allow investors to make offers on an REO property until it has been listed for sale to the public for at least two weeks.

Another hurdle when dealing with banks is what is known as a "deed restriction." This is when a bank limits you to selling the property for at most 20 percent more than your purchase price. For example, if you purchase a property for $80,000, the deed restriction will say that you're not allowed to sell it for more than $96,000. Banks also sometimes have what's called a "three-month deed restriction," which in essence means that the deed restriction (the 20 percent rule) is in effect for three months after you purchase the property, after which it no longer applies. So if you buy a property for $80,000 and you want to sell it for $100,000, you have to wait ninety days to do so. Some of these restrictions may not be revealed to you until closing day.

Now, these details are not necessarily major concerns when dealing with Section 8 properties, because Section 8 houses are typically distressed, and it can take a few months to stabilize the property between buying it, renovating it, advertising for a qualified tenant, and getting a tenant moved in. Moreover, you're planning on renting the property, so restrictions on selling it aren't a major concern.

Realtors can also help you find houses, but they are a bit of hit-and-miss as a resource because you may be battling with twenty other offers for the same property, which could create a bidding war.

Another source for housing is what's known as "short sales," which are houses that the bank has agreed to allow the mortgage-holder to sell for less than what is still owed. These sales must be approved by the lending bank, which can be a very lengthy process, taking as long as eighteen months.

Dealing with Section 8 housing is a complicated process; it's not one for the faint of heart. But if you're determined and resourceful, you can manage it yourself. Or if you're looking to invest without the daily operational dealings of property management, then property management companies offer that expertise for you.

CONCLUSION

The key to success with properties for the Section 8 program is to focus on those that give you stability and consistent results year in and year out. Your investment in properties for Section 8 tenants should be guided by the Income Trifecta, an effort to balance your investment to provide you with security, income, and liquidity. Sourcing products will also require a lot of research and footwork; it's a complicated process but one that a good management company has the resources to deal with.

CHAPTER 3 TAKEAWAYS

The Income Trifecta
1. Security: Find a home that is clearly in a livable area for a family with kids.

2. Income: Avoid going for a very inexpensive or very high-end property.

3. Liquidity: Look for homes that have the ability to attract a buyer down the road.

CHAPTER 4

THE PROS AND CONS OF INVESTING IN GOVERNMENT-SUBSIDIZED HOUSING

I t's often surprising to find out that the United States government offers assistance for people who need housing. The assumption is that everyone in America is very entrepreneurial and that people have to survive on their own; however, the reality is that one in five Americans receive some kind of government support.

As a government-backed program, it stands to reason that investors typically have a number of questions and concerns about investing in housing for Section 8 tenants. But Section 8 tenants are not necessarily risky tenants. The great majority are simply honest citizens who have qualified for Section 8 on account of their low income. This type of tenant will more often than not be at least as careful, if not more so, than a tenant who receives no government aid. Why? Because like you, the lessor, tenants must also comply to certain requirements set forth by HUD.

For example, lessors are not reimbursed for damage caused by Section 8 tenants. However, the Section 8 administration reserves the right to reduce the value of the vouchers it supplies or to terminate the tenant's participation in the program if he or she fails to keep the property in good standing. Any fraudulent behavior or breach in the contractual agreement can be a reason to be permanently removed from the program—another motivator for tenants to treat their housing well.

Similarly, proprietors must also adhere to Section 8 requirements in order to remain in the program. For example, they must maintain their houses in a habitable state during the entire period of tenancy.

With those caveats in mind, let's delve into some of the pros and cons of investing in government-subsidized housing.

THE UPSIDE OF INVESTING IN SECTION 8 HOUSING

It bears repeating that properties qualifying for the Section 8 program are not vacation homes; these houses are not typically in neighborhoods that you, the investor, would want to visit on a family trip. But, again, one of the biggest plusses of the Section 8 program is a high potential to earn more than any other type of investment.

The formula for determining the amount of subsidy paid by the government to a Section 8 property is fairly complex, so dealing with Section 8 investments is more intricate than dealing with a traditional rental property. But it's a mistake to believe that a house being used by a Section 8 tenant will automatically require more repairs or suffer more damage than a traditional rental; speaking from experience, my management company has dealt with properties left in far worse shape by traditional renters.

Section 8 properties do tend to need more attention simply because the Section 8 renters are often less versed in fixing issues that might arise. Many Section 8 renters are single mothers who have never been educated in fixing plumbing, electrical, or other issues typically handled by a professional—and the last thing you want is for a renter to attempt to make repairs on his or her own, as that could lead to more issues to repair. Keep in mind that because Section 8 houses bring in more rent than traditional homes, you'll have the extra income to help with those repairs.

In truth, there are only so many repairs a house can require, and if the only problem you face is going to the property once every three months to fix a toilet, a damaged door, or a leaky faucet, then you're coming out ahead. If you have a portfolio of homes, your overall performance of income versus repairs will far outweigh a business plan that's based on traditional tenants in those same houses.

The vast majority of Section 8 tenants renew their one-year contracts, which is not true of traditional tenants. As long as your house remains in good condition and you and your tenant respect the Section 8 criteria, the rent will be paid regularly on the first of the month. And that rent is usually higher than that received from nonsubsidized tenants.

In addition, if rental market prices go up, you can ask for a reestimate of your rental and will very likely have your request granted. If you can show that the rent for houses in your area is higher, you will likely win your case.

There are exceptions that still surprise us. For example, we had a tenant come in with a voucher for $2,400; the tenant needed a six-bedroom house, which we happened to have in inventory. We had finished that house for $88,000, and we're getting almost $30,000 of income a year on that property—a 37 percent return. Clearly, there is nothing else on the planet that will give you that kind of return.

Moreover, there is long list of candidates in the Section 8 program, and the government helps you find tenants by providing a website specifically for connecting lessors and tenants. I'll discuss more about this website later in the book.

If you're looking at this investment from outside the United States, the rent you collect is in American dollars, and those dollars can always be brought back to your country of residence to support your life or needs.

Another plus of this type of investment is the ability to build a portfolio of any size. Let's look at this by doing some reverse calculations. For example, let's say that you want to receive $5,000 a month in rent to provide you with monthly or supplemental income. If you're charging $1,300 a month in rent, then you essentially need six houses after counting in expenses throughout the year. If those are $100,000 houses, then you need to invest $600,000.

In more traditional real estate dealings, you would need to invest closer to $1 million to net $5,000 a month in rent. In Fort Lauderdale, a $1.1 million townhome rents for $5,000 per month. With a $400,000 investment in four Section 8 properties, you could afford rent on one of those townhomes and live in million-dollar conditions. Why go through all the sacrifice that it takes to buy a million-dollar property when you could live in one for a $400,000 investment?

THE RISKS OF INVESTING IN SECTION 8 HOUSING

As previously mentioned, one of the biggest concerns of investors is damage to their property. Tenants must abide by the lease that is put in place, adhering to rules such as paying rent on time, not leaving wet towels on the floor, and not parking on the grass. Rules like these are basic living standards that a lessor can require and enforce, and tenants must be informed that HUD authorities will be notified if the rules are not adhered to.

Unfortunately, as with any rental property, damage by tenants can and does happen, and damage caused by Section 8 tenants is not covered by the social aid program. However, the Section 8 administration reserves the right to cease delivering a voucher if a tenant does not respect his or her tenancy contract or fails to keep the property in good repair. Similarly, tenants found guilty of fraud (falsification of documents, for example) will be immediately struck off the list. If Section 8 tenants do not respect their contractual engagements toward the lessor or toward the terms of Section 8, they will no longer qualify for the subsidy.

This can also work in the opposite way. If a Section 8 tenant damages a property, you are still obliged to carry out repairs and to keep the house in a habitable state during the period of tenancy whether it is entirely the tenant's fault or not. This is just part of your responsibilities as lessor. If these repairs are not carried out rapidly—sometimes they must be completed within twenty-four hours—then you run the risk of having the rent subsidy eliminated altogether.

A knowledgeable property management company can help you understand and interpret landlord-tenant laws, which vary from state to state.

ABATEMENTS

As a general rule, real estate investors are looking to get the most income out of their investment while doing the least upkeep possible. This tends to work in the low-income housing market, but there is a limit to what your tenant should tolerate from your property's overall condition.

That leads us to the concept of abatements. If you fail in your responsibility of maintaining the property within the standards put forth by the PHA overseeing the properties, the PHA can suspend payments, a condition known as "abatement." Abatement in Section 8 is the equivalent of the "death penalty" in college sports. If you receive a letter from the PHA stating that you are in abatement, it means that you are in noncompliance with the program. Basically, you need to repair something or they will continue to withhold rent.

For example, if a house becomes infested with termites and the owner of the property doesn't treat the matter, the PHA has the ability to disqualify or suspend payment. This applies to items as minor as a detached shower knob that needs to be replaced; a pair of pliers being used as a knob is a dysfunction in the eyes of HUD.

When a dysfunction is found, the owner of the property is given a time frame (typically thirty days) to resolve the issue, and re-inspection is automatic. If you haven't addressed the issue by the time of the re-inspection, you immediately fall into abatement. Fixing a problem that is deemed dysfunctional is sometimes made difficult by tenants who work and aren't available to let you into the house during the day or by problematic tenants who claim to need ample warning before you enter a property. These delays make it more challenging to be in compliance and demonstrate why effective management needs to be in place. Some repairs, such as gas leaks, are required to be addressed within twenty-four hours, and you had better have the proper vendor available to identify and fix the issue within that time frame.

In our firm, the threat of abatement is top priority; it is an urgent situation. Once re-inspection determines that an abatement issue has been fixed, then rent is restored and prorated based on the re-inspection date.

There are several situations that may ultimately lead to abatement. One is when your tenant calls the PHA and reports a problem that you seem to be opposed to repairing. The PHA will then issue a special inspection to determine the issue at hand. Another situation that could lead to abatement is the re-inspection to renew your lease for twelve months. In both cases, if a repair is needed, you (as the lessor) are sent a letter notifying you that you have thirty days or less to address this particular issue. In spite of this advance warning, many lessors still fall into abatement for a couple of reasons: One, the tenant might not let you into the house, and next thing you know, the inspector has already made it back to your property to see that nothing was done; or two, the handyperson didn't complete the work as requested.

The first scenario can usually be considered a breach of the lease agreement. Avoiding this scenario comes down to your ability to communicate with your tenant about getting inside the property when it's convenient to the family.

The second scenario is about the art of delegation and the risks of low-quality handypeople. Handypeople come in many forms, but when it comes to fixing a specific issue for the PHA, you don't want to cross your fingers and wonder if the handyperson made that exact repair. Section 8 repairs require precision, skill, and follow-through; you can't allow a handyperson to cause you to lose rental income just because he or she didn't read the inspection report completely—if a professional is sent to fix three issues, he or she needs to fix those three issues.

THE RARE EVICTIONS

Despite the calculations done by the Section 8 administration, things happen to people; for example, they might lose their job as soon as they move into a property. But at the end of the day, it is very rare to be in a position where tenants don't pay us rent.

However, Section 8 tenants tend to test the waters a little more; often, they allocate some of their income to other items such as their car or cell phone, which can create a bit more of a headache in terms of collections. But this rarely escalates to the point where you're literally there with the sheriff and changing the locks because that would mean the end of their voucher. There is just too much at stake for them.

In the event of an eviction due to unpaid rent, there can be complicated cases, but overall, the laws in most states favor lessors. There's usually a process involved that requires you to start issuing three-day notices on the sixth day of the month, and after that three-day notice expires, you can file for an eviction.

Depending on the availability of the judges and courts, procedures take place pretty quickly. You're typically in a two- to six-week cycle to evict a tenant.

In Europe, the laws for removing a tenant are far more difficult and can actually make your investment property a complete nightmare, with tenants living in your property for two or three years before you can remove them. This has usually been a strong incentive for Europeans to invest in the United States.

Just as a management company's job is to get you tenants, to collect your rent, and to have the tools to fix your property, it also needs to be competent at removing tenants from your property when needed. That's why we employ eviction specialists who come to our office every month and review our collections situation to determine which tenants must be evicted. Eviction specialists have enough experience to know how a case will probably go, and they're up to date with requirements from judges or state laws. For example, there are protections to prevent lessors from evicting people who are serving in or are veterans of the US military. It's pretty painful to have an eviction case thrown out because by then you've lost a precious two or three weeks—essentially an entire month's rent.

Rest assured, cases of evicting Section 8 tenants are extremely rare simply because the leverage is there for homeowners and lessors to collect the tenant's portion of the rent even if it's somewhat late. Just like renters of traditional properties, Section 8 renters include good payers, slow payers, and bad payers. Section 8 tenants pay different portions of their rent based on their income, and a combination of strict management policies, up-front filtering, and screening of tenants provide you with higher chances of having good or slow payers rather than bad payers. Plus, Section 8 tenants must have their accounts squared up in order to move on to the next year of benefits.

So tenants have a strong incentive to pay: If an eviction is filed on a tenant, he or she is removed from the Section 8 program and left in the position of having to come up with thousands of dollars in rent on his or her own from that point forward.

As a management company, we have a database of tenants that we can search and bring in as new prospects for a property before the current tenant leaves. This is difficult for individual investors to manage, especially those who have very little free time on their hands.

The Section 8 program has accountability measures built in, which include stopgap measures that help prevent bad behaviors and protect both the tenant and the lessor.

CONCLUSION

As you can see, there are many components to consider before jumping into an investment in Section 8 housing. It's a lot like running a business, but it can be a very lucrative business if run correctly.

Owners are generally very satisfied with the Section 8 program; nevertheless, it is important to point out that any recourse against a Section 8 tenant to recoup unpaid rent is impossible. The Section 8 administration dictates the rules, and in the vast majority of cases, one simply has to accept those rules. In addition, inspections have become very strict and increasingly difficult. The risks inherent in a Section 8 tenancy should therefore not be underestimated. Nevertheless, the risk that an ordinary, nonsubsidized tenant may fail to pay rent is equally great, if not greater—especially in periods of recession when regular rental payments are not always easy for low-income families.

For these reasons, both owner and manager must carefully evaluate the risks, but of course, the final decision is up to you, the owner.

CHAPTER 4 TAKEAWAYS

- Section 8 tenants, in general, are more likely to renew their annual contracts than traditional renters.
- Rents for Section 8 properties are usually higher than that received from nonsubsidized tenants.
- There is a long list of candidates in the Section 8 program, and the government helps you find tenants by providing a website specifically for connecting lessors and tenants.
- If a Section 8 property owner does not maintain the property according to the standards put forth by the PHA, the PHA can suspend payments, a condition known as "abatement."
- Cases of evicting Section 8 tenants are extremely rare because they have a strong incentive to pay: if an eviction is filed on a tenant, he or she is removed from the Section 8 program and left in the position of having to come up with thousands of dollars in rent on his or her own from that point forward.

CHAPTER 5

FROM REHAB TO RENTAL

For decades, America has divided neighborhoods and placed communities in certain grids that define where social classes live. It's quite easy to walk around any major city in the United States and see this clear division between neighborhoods—one minute you're in a middle- to upper-class neighborhood with manicured lawns and high-end vehicles parked in driveways, and in the next minute you cross a bridge and find yourself in a rundown area with abandoned cars and a greatly reduced sense of security.

While these areas exist nearly side-by-side, there's almost a feeling of borders between them. Although nearby neighborhoods can look and feel very different, the one commonality they have is real estate. Obviously, houses in vastly different neighborhoods sell for vastly different prices, but even in the best neighborhoods, houses sometimes become distressed and can be good candidates for Section 8 tenancy. This is especially true since the housing crash.

HUD has certain standards it requires for properties to qualify for Section 8 tenants. You'll want to check with the HUD authorities in the area you're looking to invest in because the United States is a massive country with varying climates. HUD standards will require a variety of conditions to be met based on the geographic location.

Wherever the properties are located, on first walk-through, the condition of many of these properties can be downright scary. It can be hard to imagine that a property in such distressed condition can rent for any amount, much less $1,500 to $1,600.

The purpose of that first walk-through is to identify core issues the property has. These include the roof, electrical components, plumbing, air conditioning equipment, and any indication of termites. We also look at other components of a house, such as windows and areas that might be affected by high humidity or that show signs of mold.

Again, the numbers need to be worked backward. If a property is selling for $100,000 and it's going to take $20,000 to fix, but we know that we're probably going to get $1,600 in rent because it's a three/two or four/two (three- or four-bedroom house with two bathrooms). This means that ultimately, the house can be a high-performing economic product. Remember the $360,000 house I owned and couldn't keep a tenant in for $1,600? Now, that same $1,600 rent is earned from a $120,000 property—this is real estate that pays.

Again, we've found that the ideal properties are those three- or four-bedroom houses with two bathrooms; even a three-bedroom house with a garage converted to a fourth bedroom often makes a good candidate. We shy away from other forms of real estate because single-family homes are in greater demand and generally offer the greatest return on investment. We will take on duplexes simply because they offer the chance to always have a tenant providing income; if a tenant in one unit moves out, the other tenant is usually still there. But the numbers need to make sense in terms of making a property functional and obtaining the correct rent. While there are some advantages of townhomes in the form of maintenance guarantees, insurance, and other common-law protections, we tend to stay away from them; homeowner's association fees can take a big bite out of the rent, especially on top of fees applied by a management company.

When it comes to the resale of a property in the future, single-family homes are the clear winner due to the fact that they generate more rent and traditionally offer more space. There will always be a much wider market of people who want single-family homes for their families rather than townhomes.

REPAIRING A PROPERTY

Managing repairs is one of the more challenging aspects of investing in real estate. If you are an individual investor with only one house, then you know that it can be very difficult to find reliable help. If you've ever tried to get help for home repairs, then you've probably encountered an industry of workers who are often financially insecure. Many cannot perform quality work without constant supervision, and others leave tasks incomplete; it's a common-sense-free atmosphere where you end up with what I call the 80/20 rule—80 percent of the house is completed in three days, and the remaining 20 percent takes two weeks.

As a management company, we have access to professionals in the different trades that are required: plumbing, electrical, air conditioning, roofing, and so forth. We have the volume of new and existing properties to keep repair workers busy. Plus, we've been fortunate enough to build relationships over time with some reliable and knowledgeable contractors who truly understand the ins and outs of HUD housing standards.

But even we still struggle with the 80/20 rule at times, often because we're waiting on parts or other problems we found once work started on a house. With our volume, we're in an endless race of trying to finish houses in time for inspection. As an investor or real estate entrepreneur, the last thing you want is a two- or three-week delay in getting a tenant into a house; that's just throwing away rental income.

It's also important to note that the need for repairs does not stop once a rental is move-in ready. You may have had beautiful weather for three weeks while repairing the house, but if it rains the day a tenant moves in, you may find that the property has a leaky roof. It can be discouraging to have a tenant call right away and list off seven items that aren't up to par, but that's the nature of the business. There are houses that just require repetitive visits for repairs, which is why having a reliable and knowledgeable handyperson is key; you want someone who can look at a roof and realize that a leak is imminent.

We're always amazed at the number of tenants who want to move into our properties because their previous lessor wouldn't keep up with repairs. There are a lot of lessors out there who don't want to spend money on repairs, which leads to tenants leaving. But as I've mentioned, our philosophy is that you should take care of the tenants no matter what. It leads to tenant retention, which is the cheapest and easiest way to optimize your income in the long term.

Once you've landed a property, the first step in rehabbing it is to get the utilities—electricity and water—connected. Several times, we've been in situations where electricity was not present at the property; the property had been stripped of its wiring. An instance like this requires permits, an electrician to reinstall an electrical panel, and meetings with city inspectors to get approval for the reinstallation of a meter. This can be a two- to three-week process, which slows you down tremendously when you're trying to get the entire house turned around in that same time frame. Often, multiple steps must occur just to get power in the house; without electricity, you can't renovate a property unless you have battery-operated tools and a generator. Those are not ideal ways to work and prepare a property.

Once your repair teams clearly understand what it takes to get a house up to Section 8 standards, then there are a number of visits and estimates needed to reach an agreement on the work to be done. These include decisions on whether to repair or replace components required to make the house functional and to ultimately pass an inspection. You'll find that some properties require very little work, while others may need seemingly everything from the roof on down. If a roof is needed, it's typically the first thing that needs to be done before you can even consider what to repair on the rest of the house.

Again, you'll need to reach out to different vendors depending on what needs to be done and in what order. For example, you won't call in the painters first, but you may want to get an early estimate and get a crew lined up for later down the road—for example, after the roof is on and the sheetrock has been replaced or repaired.

In addition to the roof and utilities, there are other components that must pass inspection: windows must be able to open and close and must be screened, bathrooms must be vented, appliances must function properly, electrical outlets must be grounded, doors must be weather-stripped, the water heater must have a release valve, there cannot be any cracked or sharp-edged tiles, and baseboards must be firmly in place. The list goes on. For example, a critical item on an inspector's list is functional smoke detectors—either battery operated or hardwired.

Aesthetically, the property must be clean and painted. The yard must be free of debris—no large rocks, bricks, or other hindrances—and if there is a pool on the property, it must be properly fenced to avoid a toddler from falling in.

After you've rehabilitated a few of these properties, you'll develop a system. You'll become skilled at identifying some basic pieces needed in a property, you'll begin to cement the costs of repairs in your mind, and you'll determine which resources you'll allocate toward a property. Soon, you'll be able to estimate when a product will be finished, allowing for any unexpected issues. And when a property is ready, you'll know that a tenant will make it their new residence and that you can expect rent from them each month.

The following are some of the issues that must be addressed, whether rehabilitating a house for the first time or renewing a lease after a Section 8 tenant has been in the property for one year. My cost estimates are for Florida, but they should serve as a good guideline for many other areas of the United States.

 • **Termite treatment:** Termites can appear at any time and must be treated as quickly as possible to avoid a suspension of rent payments from the housing authorities. Depending on the number and location of the termites, you may be required to hire a specialized company to cover the house with a fumigation tent. This costs around $700 to $900, depending on the size of the house. In addition to that expense, it is often necessary to put the family up in a hotel for two or three nights at a cost of approximately $300. There may also be additional labor costs for treating any structure attached to the house.

- **Nonfunctioning air conditioning or furnaces:** Florida heat puts a lot of stress on air conditioning units every day of the year. This causes wear and tear over time, sometimes requiring the replacement of certain parts. Depending on the size of the existing unit, the replacement cost can reach around $3,700 for a full installation. More often, basic maintenance must be performed to the coil; this costs approximately $250 and can happen up to twice a year in the worst cases. In colder climates such as Detroit, furnaces wear out more quickly and cost around $2,000 to fully replace.

- **Roof leaks:** A roof leak must be fixed because it can quickly become a cause for concern. Roof patches cost approximately $400, while repairing a larger section of roof can cost around $1,500. It's important to address this early in Florida because it is such a rainy region; damage caused by water can result in far more costly repairs on a house.

- **Pool maintenance:** A pool is often a part of the house that needs to be maintained by the owner, something foreign investors are not accustomed to. However, the tenants who most often live in the type of investment properties that we manage are not knowledgeable enough to treat the pool regularly or lack sufficient means to do so. Regular, monthly treatment is required and can cost up to $95 per month. Other maintenance issues can also occur, such as filter replacements(about $90–$120) or a pool pump replacement (approximately $400). In Florida, an unmaintained pool turns green very quickly, which causes a health hazard for the family living at the home and can lead to city fines and penalties.

 • **Lawn care:** Lawn care has become one of the requirements the city is most vigilant about. City officials spend their days driving through the streets to identify unmaintained properties. Once found, they post a warning letter on the door of the property and send a certified letter to the registered owner. Our leases typically require tenants to cut the lawn themselves, but for some negligent tenants, we employ a lawn service in order to avoid city fines. A standard lawn cut costs approximately $30–$40; hedge trimming or tree pruning can also incur additional fees.

 • **Plumbing issues:** Plumbing problems can range from minor to major, but even minor water damage must be taken seriously, as it can lead to bigger problems, including mold. Mold is the most common source of legal issues with tenants, as they often claim respiratory issues with their children or damage to their personal property. It is therefore essential to handle plumbing issues quickly. The costs of such repairs vary; they can range from $150 to $3,000, depending on the quantity of work required. Some instances have required the removal of entire walls, which creates the need to buy additional materials to bring the property back to its original condition. One worst-case instance includes digging under the property to replace a broken line or one that has been infiltrated by tree roots, which often cause major backup into the property. This type of situation can cost up to $10,000. Some properties have septic tanks; these must be emptied, and on occasion the drain fields must be replaced. Replacement of a drain field costs around $3,000, and replacement of a septic tank pump costs around $250 to $300. A septic-to-sewer connection is also approximately $3,000 and can be required by the city if there is a municipal order for such infrastructure upgrades.

• **Small plumbing issues:** The leases that tenants agree to require them to be responsible for small plumbing issues such as backed-up toilets, faucet leaks, and leaks underneath sinks. However, due to the nature of Section 8 tenants, we often use our services to attend to these small plumbing issues. Even when we suspect that the tenant is responsible for the problem, we address the issue to avoid a tenant complaint to the PHA, which would lead to an official inspection. As the management company, we charge both the owner of the property and the tenant for this service in an effort to get the tenant to reimburse the owner as part of their lease obligation. This is the most common expense that we battle, and it can range from $100 and $250 with each occurrence.

• **Vandalism:** Most instances of vandalism occur when a property is vacant. The extent of the damage varies, but it ranges from stolen appliances to structural damage, such as broken doors or windows or stolen copper components. The cost of repairs varies but can be as severe as $5,000. Most often, damage is caused by a break-in, and although insurance covers vandalism, the damage is commonly less than the deductible.

- **Electrical issues:** Modern families use more electricity than many of these homes were designed for, so on occasion, a meter or other electrical component must be upgraded. This requires the services of an electrician, and costs are always the responsibility of the owner of the property.

- **Utilities:** Utilities are, unless specified in the lease, the tenant's responsibility. However, at the time of a move-out, the property needs to be cleaned and repaired in order to pass inspection for the new family moving in. This requires water and electrical to be connected during the period of vacancy, as an inspector must ensure that such components of the house work properly. As soon as an inspection is passed, we ask the new tenant to connect under his or her name because the electric company charges a standard connection fee of approximately $15, and a monthly bill is sent to our offices until a new tenant connects. Utility expenses during a vacancy can cost $200–$500.

- **Appliances:** Sometimes appliances malfunction, which can cause tenants real concern; for example, a malfunctioning refrigerator can lead to spoilage of perishable foods. We use the services of an appliance specialist for repairs; however, some repairs can exceed the cost of replacing an appliance. Appliances range from $130 to $250. In order to limit this expense, we no longer offer washers and dryers as part of a lease.

RELATIONSHIPS WITH INSPECTORS

I can't stress enough the importance of having good relationships with inspectors when dealing with Section 8. These relationships come from building a reputation for following the rules and doing what you say you'll do.

My company has been at this long enough to prove ourselves honest and worthy to inspectors. For example, if there's a missing screen or an appliance isn't functioning like we expected after it was installed, then we're able to send a text message to the inspector with a photo of the receipt and the repair or the new appliance in place. The inspectors we've worked a lot with in the past don't want us to slow down; they trust us to get the work done, and we do. First-time investors rarely get that kind of a pass.

Keep in mind, your property doesn't necessarily have to be in perfect condition. It's not uncommon for an inspector to have six or a dozen inspections in one day, so they're often in a hurry to get through a property. If they know you well and know your work and your standards, they may move through the property fairly quickly and pass on some of the less critical items. It's a victory every time we pass inspection because that leads to the ultimate goal—getting a family into the house.

Everyone in real estate wants to pass inspection, whether you're getting a city inspection or a Section 8 inspection. So when you show up at the property and the inspector is there, you must be on your best behavior—it's like examination day. If you've delegated the preparation of this house to your contractor and haven't necessarily been to the property on a consistent basis to check on the progress, then you're left crossing your fingers every time you do a walk-through—that's when you'll find out if there was an oversight.

So we've implemented a pre-inspection: The day before the inspection, we do a walk-through to double- and triple-check everything. This allows us to clear the majority of the issues that may have been overlooked. Even as long as we've been at this, we often find at the last minute something staring us right in the face that we didn't realize was a problem that won't pass the inspection.

Sometimes, you'll have an inspector point out something that's never been an issue before—it may be something that previously passed dozens of inspections, but for whatever reason, this time it causes your inspection to fail, and you have to take care of it immediately.

It's back to that 80/20 rule I mentioned earlier, where the repair crew has done about 80 percent of the work, and after you visit with them they do another 80 percent of the 20 percent that's left, leaving you with about 4 percent of the overall work incomplete. Most of the time, you'll pass inspection, but there will be a small percentage of inspections that the house won't pass because of that 4 percent of work that wasn't finished.

Again, some inspectors are fairly flexible if they know you and if they understand that you have the resources and the manpower to fix outstanding problems that same day. Whenever possible, I also recommend having the contractor who oversaw the work on the property on hand during the inspection. Not only is it a good idea to have someone ready to fix whatever the inspector finds, but you're also dealing with the person who should know the house the best and who was paid to complete the work on the property.

Another reason for keeping up with housing quality standards is that Section 8 leases are renewed on a yearly basis, and an official inspection takes place at that time, encompassing checks inside and outside the property. This can result in a list of repairs that need to be done within a specified time frame before a second renewal inspection is done to officially validate the lease for an additional twelve months. The inspection report includes the lists of issues to repair—one for the tenant and one for the owner.

RELATIONSHIPS WITH CASE/ SOCIAL WORKERS

Case workers, or social workers, are linchpins in the Section 8 system. These professionals are hired by different local agencies and are assigned a quantity of vouchers. Part of their role is to collect crucial information from tenants to determine whether they qualify for Section 8 housing. Social workers are also assigned to monitor existing tenants, looking at their income and their family composition, including the children who are turning eighteen and are moving out of the property.

Section 8 vouchers are calculated by income, number of dependents, and other factors, and these can vary over time. Section 8 vouchers determine what portion of rent Section 8 pays and what portion the tenant is responsible for. This is one of the most challenging pieces of this type of investment; you must vigilantly monitor incoming mail to know when a tenant's portion has changed. In our office, we have specific staff members who monitor the mail for these notices. We also have property management software that fills in the amount that Section 8 pays and the amount that the tenant pays for rent. These figures change, and your records must be adjusted accordingly, or you may end up in a dispute with your tenant.

Sometimes, payment disputes mean dealing with tenants who claim that they're in the process of being recertified and social workers whose records may not be up to date. When this happens you're inevitably in a holding pattern, and you must reach out to the social worker to confirm that the recertification is taking place so that the rent can be properly adjusted before the tenant becomes delinquent.

For the vast majority of tenants, there are no fluctuations and everything runs pretty smoothly. With these tenants, the only time a social worker really gets involved is when it comes time to renew the lease, which is sixty days prior to the lease ending. At that time, there is a requirement to produce what's called a "request for tenancy." A "request for tenancy" is basically a request to continue a lease and to engage in the aforementioned annual inspection, which certifies the property to be Section 8 for another year. Social workers also oversee the process of dealing with special inspections when a tenant calls to report that a lessor has been reticent about fixing a reported problem.

Unfortunately, there are tenants who treat their social workers more or less like 9-1-1; they know that they hold the wild card— the simple phrase, "I'm calling housing." These are often the people who don't really have anything, so you, as the lessor, can't really take anything away from them.

Suffice it to say, good relationships with social workers can be a great benefit when it comes to issues like renewing a lease or when tenants decide to move to another property. Conversely, being on bad terms with your Section 8 case worker can be a real disadvantage; you may find them siding with tenants more often, even if the tenant is in the wrong.

CONCLUSION

An important message that I'll repeat throughout the book is that the name of the game is *tenant retention*. That is the top driver of your return on investment. If you refuse to fix things or impose on your tenants to spend their money on repairs—especially those things you know you should be paying for—you take the risk of them moving to another, newly renovated, operational property right down the street from yours—a property owned by a different lessor who will be more than happy to collect the steady, monthly income.

The ultimate goal is to support the needs of tenants because consistent income, higher collections, and higher return on investment are all linked together. From performing due diligence and repairing properties to HUD standards and forging industry relationships, it takes time and a real sense of organization to succeed with Section 8. As you gain experience, you'll better understand the ins and outs of the Section 8 program, but it will always remain challenging—and rewarding.

CHAPTER 5 TAKEAWAYS

Issues to Address to Qualify a Property for the Section 8 Program

- termite treatment
- nonfunctioning air conditioning or furnaces
- roof leaks
- pool maintenance
- lawn care
- plumbing issues
- small plumbing issues
- vandalism
- electrical issues
- utilities
- appliances

CHAPTER 6

BUILDING YOUR NEST EGG

As an investor in real estate, you are, in essence, a small business, and there are a lot of details to consider with the business aspects of rental investments. Working through the calculations and paperwork is a crucial piece of investing in rental properties for the Section 8 program. This chapter will discuss those calculations as well as tips for finding and placing tenants.

THE 65/35 RULE

Once you have an idea of the voucher amounts available to you, you can sculpt a business plan around those figures. Based on your level of investment, start by identifying how many properties you need to have in order to get a specific dollar amount every month.

Let's say that you want to add $5,000 of supplemental income to your current life, either in addition to your professional activities or as a source of income to live on. If you know that three-bedroom vouchers in your area pay $1,200 dollars, how much money will you need to invest to receive $5,000 per month? Basic math would tell you that four or five properties are needed to accomplish this.

But as a general rule, our experience shows that your investment will have an income-to-expense ratio of 65/35. This means that your $5,000 income goal over twelve months would give you a total of $60,000, but in reality you will obtain around $39,000 of net income. So if you plan on averaging $5,000 per month over the span of twelve months, then you'll need $92,307 in total rent to achieve a net return of $60,000. That $60,000 is 65 percent of $92,307, which when divided by twelve months gives you a monthly gross rent of $7692.25—that's the monthly gross rent that you need to collect in order to net an average of $5,000 per month.

Now let's look at the original investment amount. If we consider that a $110,000, three/two (three beds, two baths) home provides you $1,200 a month in rent, that means you will need just under eight properties (eight properties times $1,200). With the investment per home being $110,000, then you need to spend approximately $880,000.

This calculation is valid for any investor, whether you want to have $1,000 or $20,000 in rent each month. $880,000 may be a lot for some investors, but you can scale it down to your needs.

As you go through this plan, it's important to be aware of the expenses that are attached to real estate. A property is essentially "alive and kicking" every day; wear and tear on the property will result in sometimes-volatile upkeep expenses. For example, a family of three or four people is going to open the front door probably fifteen times a day.

So what compromises that 35 percent of expenses that you should have as a golden rule?

- property taxes
- management fees/leasing fees
- repairs
- rental certificates with the city (business license)
- accountant
- insurance
- income taxes

In addition to general upkeep, you have property taxes, which can cost you almost two months of rent in most cases. In the United States, property taxes range from 1 percent to 2 percent of the value of the asset. This value is estimated annually by the county appraiser.

Property taxes are a once-per-year expense that you simply have to pay. Your property taxes allow the municipality to provide roads, schools, and many other services. We won't go into that detail in this book, as most investors understand this expense to be necessary and standard. In Florida, you pay these expenses starting in November, and there is actually a 4 percent discount if you do so. The discount falls to 3 percent in December, 2 percent in January, and 1 percent in February, and there is no discount in March. Most people take advantage of the 4 percent discount rate, as this is all about efficiency and income optimization. In some states, like Michigan, you will have a summer and winter tax paid at different times of the year.

Regardless of the state, property taxes are mandatory, and if they are not paid, the government can seize your property.

Municipalities have what's called a "millage" rate, which is the rate at which property taxes are levied. The millage rate can be different from one city to another even when the product is the same. For example, a three/two (three bedroom, two bath) in Fort Lauderdale might have a property tax of $1,400, but a three/two just a few miles away might be $2,200.

Let's calculate an example of expenses using the 65/35 ratio. Consider that you have one house that rents for $1,300. That monthly rent multiplied by twelve months equals $15,600 in rent per year. Multiply that by 0.35 (35 percent), and you end up with $5,460 in expenses per year on that house.

In addition, if you have a management company in place, then your management fees will consume 10 to 12 percent of your income. I'll expand on the management fees in an upcoming chapter.

FINANCING YOUR VENTURE

As I've said, Section 8 investments are ideal for cash investors; the previous number-crunching exercise is for investors who are paying cash for their properties. Our investors have predominately been people who have liquidity, and we initially focused on people who had money sitting in the bank.

But there are different ways to finance investments. If you're an international investor, you might have assets in your country or elsewhere that you can use as collateral for a loan to buy properties in America.

If you're an American, you might go through traditional financing, which includes a down payment and financing the rest of the cost using a loan with preferred rates that allow you to create leverage. If you have $100,000, instead of spending it on one house, you might be able to put $20,000 to $30,000 down on each of three or four houses. Then you're growing your portfolio; you're looking for the market to go up and allow your assets to increase in value with the minimum amount of money invested.

Look at your investment from a cash-on-cash basis; once you've paid your mortgage, you're left with X amount of dollars per month, and if you add that dollar amount up over twelve months, how does that compare to the money that you invested? You might have only spent $20,000 but, at the end of the year, after the mortgage and other expenses, you might have $6,000 left in the bank, and $6,000 over $20,000 is an excellent cash-on-cash return. There are not a lot of people that invest $20,000 and get $6,000 out of it after a year.

These days, some financial institutions offer property management companies a chance to refinance the investors that they manage. If the financial institutions feel secure about property management companies that are in control of their business and their tenants, they approve refinancing certain investors that have paid cash for their property. Refinancing allows those investors to buy extra property with the understanding that the management company has an eye on the tenants at all times and has the ability to secure the income and, therefore, cover the mortgage payments to those financial institutions.

This is huge. It allows management companies to go back to investors and offer to take 60 to 65 percent of the $500,000 they have invested and use it to purchase another three or four houses. This offer is not available to the traditional investor; it's only available to investors who work within a network of property management companies that have been credited or approved to offer this financial product.

FORMING THE BUSINESS

When acquiring properties, we recommend that you form a limited liability company (LLC). Most of the time, this business structure is set up in the state in which the house or the investor is located.

It is of interest to overseas investors that investments on rented property in the United States are controlled by bilateral taxation agreements with your country of residence, which allow this type of investment to be taxed in the United States. In order to avoid double taxation, a tax credit is attributed in the country of residence, with tax authorities reserving the right to carry out income tax readjustments. The advantage in terms of United States taxation are the deductions related to property management that I mentioned earlier in the book, one round-trip airfare per year to the United States, and a personal exemption of nearly $4,000 for each foreign member of the LLC.

For example, if you have $14,000 of rental income and a personal exemption of $4,000, then you are taxed based on an income of $10,000, not $14,000. If you have another member in the LLC, then you shave off another $4,000. However, keep in mind that the tax credit for investors is per individual; if you have ten houses, you still only get one personal exemption.

To set up an LLC, you must first check to see that the name you want for your LLC is available; this is usually fairly simple to check online. Often, the investors we work with like to use the street address as the LLC. If they are buying 2300 Central Street, then the name of the company would be 2300 Central Street, LLC.

For American investors, an LLC protects your personal assets by surrounding your investment with a corporate shell that cannot be pierced; this prevents your other personal assets from being subject to litigation if the LLC is under legal attack.

As a foreign investor, there is a withholding of 10 percent of the sale price at the time of closing, but this is not required if you are under an LLC format. Recovering the funds from this withholding requires a series of steps with an accountant and the Internal Revenue Service (IRS) and can be a lengthy process. An LLC allows you to be considered as a United States person, which lets you more readily collect the proceeds of your sale when that time comes.

The number of members in an LLC is unlimited. Usually, our investors have two members, but some have four or five members including children over the age of eighteen who have been added to the LLC. For a small additional cost, the state of Delaware allows the establishment of an LLC without revealing to the public who its members are, providing investors and business owners with extra privacy compared to other states.

There is also an annual cost for renewing an LLC, which depends on the state the LLC is in. This expense is typically incurred between January and May and is part of your annual expenses to account for on your profit-and-loss statement.

After the LLC is created, generally a deposit is put down on the property with the title company handling the closing. Industry standards usually ask for $5,000 to secure a property. This deposit financially engages the buyer and is usually a requirement to have the contract on the property executed.

Foreign investors need to have a bank account in the United States to deal with these properties. In the United States, there are innumerable national and international banks, so a foreign investor can set up an account and have easy access to his or her funds to issue transfers or simply park money.

The title company responsible for the closing will provide a series of documents including the amount of money owed to complete the purchase, basic disclosures, buyer's documents, and affidavits. The title company then waits for the money transfer to arrive and notifies both parties. Once the purchase has been completed, the title company follows a procedure that will process the recording of your acquisition electronically a few days later.

FINDING TENANTS

Now that you have secured your investment, you need to find those Section 8 tenants. Luckily, the government is on your side and has designed a website specifically for that purpose: www.gosection8. com.

This site is extremely friendly to both tenants and lessors. Tenants can access the site and see properties you have listed along with comments and pictures. They can also contact you by e-mail or phone to schedule a visit. The website gives you daily updates of the attention your properties are getting, and it provides you with the number of possible matches that could be a fit for your houses. It's almost like a dating website for your house. I view it as a major part of the Income Trifecta I discussed earlier because it provides the security of knowing that thousands of prospective tenants are at your fingertips anytime.

Our company has twenty to thirty houses advertised on www.gosection8.com at all times, and it's fair to say that our leasing agents receive one hundred phone calls a day. If you decide to go with Section 8 tenants, get ready for the phone to ring and for properties to be shown. These calls come in at all times of the day, so plan on your voicemail being filled with requests.

You also need to develop a system to manage all the new tenants who want to view your properties. When I first began this venture, I drove from one property to another with my phone ringing nonstop. As a result, I developed a system to retain prospects' phone numbers; I would immediately rename them in my phone with a reference to the property address. But I also decided it was important to classify them by voucher amounts so I could identify the best possible scenarios for each property.

For example, if my property address was 1230 and a tenant just called me with a $1,200 voucher and an April 1 move-in date, I would rename the number "1230 Stephanie 1200 April 1st." April 1 was a key date to record because each prospect was organizing their move-in day, which didn't necessarily correspond to my move-in day.

Oftentimes I had several tenants looking to move into one property, so it felt like I was missing out on tenants because I didn't have houses for them. That's the worst feeling—wishing you had a huge bank account with the power to buy dozens of new homes just to fit these tenants in somewhere. But remember that tenants who I couldn't take in the following month were either going to find another property or renew with their current lessor when their lease ends. Tenants have to provide a sixty-day notice before leaving, which meant that I may very easily have a new tenant for that 1230 property in ten months if my current tenant decides to move.

Tenants who are unsatisfied with their current housing will naturally consider their options, so it's important to maintain a pipeline of prospects. The name of the game is keeping your house occupied, and that takes clear organization. But with today's smartphones, you have some basic tricks that let you file your prospects by property. If you have a lot of properties, I recommend getting a separate smartphone just for this purpose; otherwise, you'll find it a little strange to have 75 percent of your contact list be tenant prospects rather than friends and family.

QUALIFYING TENANTS, COLLECTING RENT

As I mentioned early on, in order to qualify for Section 8, a tenant's income must be below 50 percent of the national median income. Currently, that equates to earning less than $25,000. If they meet the criteria, tenants are eligible to apply with their local agency to either be provided with a voucher to move into a property immediately or to be placed on a waiting list until a certain number of existing tenants become no longer qualified for the program, allowing new tenants to be subsidized.

Once you have made an agreement with a prospective tenant to move forward, you need what I call a Section 8 Business Toolkit. This toolkit includes the paperwork from the PHA, usually called a landlord package. This is the first set of documents that you must fill out to initiate the process that gets your tenant in the house. This paperwork allows you to get paid through direct deposit, if you choose; the absolute best feeling as a lessor is getting your rents deposited electronically. The landlord package also has you specify many things about the property such as its year of construction and the size and type of property that you are renting to Section 8 tenants. Other disclaimers are there for you to check regarding lead paint, termites, radon gas, etc.

The forms also require you to clarify who is responsible for what, similar to a lease but more specific to utilities and appliances. You and your tenant must sign these documents, or the social worker assigned to your case will not process the files. The documents also contain the rent amount and the breakdown of who pays what—HUD pays X amount, and the tenant pays Y amount.

The drawback to these documents is that you usually don't get them until the third week or so after the tenant has moved into the property. Unfortunately, this can leave you with a collection issue at the beginning of the lease, because if you are trying to collect in the third week, the tenant will need to have been responsible enough to put aside sufficient money to cover his or her portion of that first month's rent right before it's time to collect for the second month. So quite often, at the start of a contract or lease, you're collecting for both the first and second months.

The way we resolve this is to try to identify what this person's portion of the rent was in his or her previous homes. If the tenant tells us that his or her portion of the rent in previous houses was $163, we try to collect a similar amount on the day that he or she moves into our property. This at least gives the tenant credit toward the rent for that month. If the tenant's portion turns out to be the amount already paid, then everything is good to go. If the tenant has paid less than his or her actual portion, then we collect more in the second month. If tenant has paid more than his or her portion, then we carry the balance into the second month as a credit toward that month's rent. For the most part, tenants know that they owe a portion of the rent, and they come through as required.

Payments can be made in a variety of ways. Some lessors show up in person to collect rent and other provide tenants with a bank account to deposit into. If you're using a management company, tenants typically drop off the payment there in the form of cash, a money order, or if the company doesn't prohibit it, a check. Today, some types of property management software provide tenants with the ability to pay their rent at certain retail outlets using a barcode that you supply or that they receive on their smartphone. This is scanned when they pay their rent at the participating retail outlet, and the money is deposited directly into a rent escrow account set up for that purpose.

At my firm, collections typically take place at the beginning of the month. After a set amount of time, usually around the seventh day of the month, we issue three-day notices to those tenants who have not paid. It's a one-day-a-month task that we have people assigned to, and it is to warn tenants in a consistent fashion that they are delinquent on their rent and have three days to comply.

This three-day notice is a document with a list of different reasons that are checked off depending on the scenario involved; these range from being late on rent to tenants extending their stay in a property past the lease date. The latter of these is often because the property a tenant is moving to is not ready or hasn't passed inspection. Whatever the case, we maintain a watchful eye on the terms of the lease and rent collected.

Depending on the location of your property and which agency your tenant is part of, it is quite common to have somewhat of a payment delay during the first few months of the lease. This is because social workers have a pile of folders on their desks and have to make sure that each contract and landlord package is filled out correctly before they can forward it to the accounting department.

This can be a disappointing time for owners, as they are eager to receive their rents; but once you know this detail, it becomes routine and simply requires a little patience.

It doesn't hurt to call the housing department and talk to the social worker in hopes that he or she will be able to move your file to the top of the pile. But keep in mind that social workers are human and can be quite busy with new candidates and several processes that they have to follow.

We have identified certain locations where the PHA is not worth working with due to serious delays in their payment processing. We decided to simply avoid those locations altogether—there is no point in waiting six months for your rents to come in, especially if you have repairs, mortgages, or your property taxes to pay.

The goal is to work with agencies that have an efficient payment processing system, which usually means that you get paid by the second month, and from that point on the rents come in at the beginning of the month. We all agree that it's worth waiting one month to get your rents and then have them come in automatically.

CONCLUSION

There are a lot of details to consider when financing a house, dealing with paperwork, and finding Section 8 tenants. Once you've found your property, setting up an LLC can help protect your other interests. I've also included in this chapter a few tips for collecting rent—one of the most worrisome tasks many lessors face.

Next, let's look at some of the fiscal advantages associated with the Section 8 program, for both American and overseas investors.

CHAPTER 6 TAKEAWAYS

- Begin creating a business plan by identifying how many properties you need to have in order to earn a specific dollar amount each month.
- As a general rule, your investment will have an income to expense ratio of 65/35.
- Section 8 investments are ideal for cash investors, but investors can also use collateral or obtaining traditional financing.
- Foreign investors should ensure their investments are controlled by bilateral taxation agreements with their country of residence.
- Investors should form a limited liability company (LLC) in order to take advantage of the available tax benefits the designation offers.

CHAPTER 7

UNCLE SAM

Real estate in the Unites States has always been positioned by the IRS as a place to put your money and benefit from numerous advantages. That's one reason why real estate is such a popular investment. As an investor and a property owner, you're able to deduct expenses off your income for the purpose of taxes because owning real estate is running a business and involves expenses in order to function properly.

We talked about upkeep on your property. Keep in mind that upkeep repairs come in two types: general repairs and capital improvements. These are categorized differently from a fiscal standpoint. General repairs involve any repair related to the functioning of the property, such as the repair of a faucet, pest control, or (in some cases) lawn care. Capital improvements, on the other hand, are larger repairs such as a new roof, electrical panel, appliances, air conditioning unit, or windows. These depreciate over a period of years.

Every business venture has expenses; they come in different forms based on what activity you are involved in. If you are reading this and own a business, you know that this is about sustaining your ability to perform and provide results every day. It's no different in real estate; you have expenses that you simply can't avoid. We discussed the fact that the ideal ratio to attain in our $100,000 properties is 65/35 income/expense ratio. Within those expenses are items spent to run your business. With these business expenses, you essentially get to deduct every penny to lower your tax liability. Some of the more common tax-deductible business expenses claimed on tax returns include the following:

- advertising
- auto and travel expenses
- cleaning and maintenance
- commissions
- depreciation
- insurance
- legal and other professional fees
- management fees
- mortgage interest paid to banks
- repairs
- real estate taxes
- utilities

You can also reduce your tax liability by taking advantage of depreciation. Essentially, the IRS depreciates your property for twenty-seven and a half years. This means that, fiscally speaking, your property is losing value every year. At the end of twenty-seven and a half years, your property is considered to be worth zero. Of course, it's not. Its value is just decreasing every year on your tax return, which reduces your tax liability.

The majority of our investors are able to justify enough ordinary necessary expenses that they have a taxable loss for the year, giving them the ability to not pay income tax. This is the big advantage of investing in the United States; a large number of deductions are applicable on the received income, reducing taxable net income. For foreign investors, this allows you to avoid any tax repercussions in your country of residence.

As an American investor, you'll deal directly with your own accountant to ensure that your taxes are filed. If you are working with a management company, you should receive a profit-and-loss statement to provide to your accountant along with other documents to prove any other expenses that you are claiming.

For foreign investors, my company relies on the assistance of an accounting firm to handle all the details with the IRS. Our office provides the accountant with a profit-and-loss statement at the end of the year along with tax credits, depreciation, travel expenses, and any other qualifying deductible expenses, which allows us to file tax returns for our investors without them having to be present.

We've found that the services of an accountant vary greatly, costing from $250 to $1,000 for the same service. So it's a good idea to shop around a little for a quality, not overly expensive accounting firm. There's no point in going through all the trouble to have good returns with Section 8 properties only to have an account make an unnecessary dent in that income.

What you should be paying in taxes varies greatly and is based on how you set up your investment. For example, if you've invested as a couple or if there are two or more members in your LLC, then you file what's called a partnership return as well as individual tax returns, which means that you will incur additional accountant expenses. If you're set up as an individual, then you will only have your individual tax return to file (including the net income generated by the LLC), which will produce only one bill from the accountant.

Single-member LLCs are taxed like a sole proprietorship, so the tax returns are due and taxes are payable for the prior year on April 15. A partnership return is filed as an information return on Form 1065, and tax is due on the individual partners' tax returns. Form 1065 is due on fifteenth day of the fourth month after the end of the partnership's tax year. For matters of simplicity, all of our investors have a fiscal year ending December 31, making the deadline for filing returns April 15. Multiple-member LLCs are taxed as partnerships, so the partnership filing and payment regulations previously mentioned apply, including the April 15 filing date. If an extension is filed, then the return is due October 15.

Realistically, if you're in a 10 percent tax bracket and when all is said and done you have $3,000 taxable income, then you're going to pay $300. If you have $14,000 income, then you would pay $1,400. In addition to the previously mentioned tax advantages for foreign investors, there is also a one-time tax credit of nearly $4,000. So every time you have a $4,000 credit, you're basically shaving $400 off your tax liability. If you have two foreign members of the LLC, you're technically shaving $800 off your tax liability. And $800, in many cases, is three-quarters of a month of rent. For foreign buyers, there is clearly a message here.

LAND TRUSTS

Another way to protect the owner or owners of a property is through a land trust. A land trust is usually used to buy a property, and you can have one or multiple properties in a single land trust.

A land trust is an arrangement by which the recorded title to the real estate is held by a trustee, but all the rights and conveniences of ownership are exercised by the beneficiary, whose interest is not disclosed. The trustee is not liable for anything in the land trust.

The main advantage of using a land trust is complete confidentiality for the beneficiary. Issues can only be addressed to the trustee, whose role is to serve as administrator of the trust and to relay any correspondence or information about the trust to the beneficiary. Although the beneficiary is the owner of the trust, he or she can resign as having the beneficial interests of the property and can provide to a new beneficiary the ownership over the trust.

With land trusts, there are significant advantages for inheritance purposes. For example, you can name a successor beneficiary. That way, if the beneficiary were to lose his or her life, the successor beneficiary could just take over the trust, and the property wouldn't have to go through probate. Land trusts provide a huge tax advantage for foreign investors to set up a succession strategy that can optimize tax liability down the road.

There are only a few states that allow the title of the property to be under the name of a land trust, a feature that many of our investors have opted for. Land trusts allow us to provide our investors with a way to optimize their confidentiality needs and their inheritance strategies.

As mentioned, we always recommend buying your house through an LLC. If you've decided to buy property in the name of a land trust, the LLC becomes the beneficiary of the land trust. Again, the land trust offers you confidentiality, and the LLC offers you protection.

CRUNCHING THE NUMBERS

When you buy real estate, depending on what part of the world you are in, closing costs can vary quite a bit. Foreign investors are used to paying much higher fees than in the United States. It's not uncommon to see closing costs in Europe around the 10 percent range, made worse by the fact that they are actually paid by the buyer.

In the United States, closing costs are paid by both parties—the buyer and seller—and on the buyer's end, they're usually between 1.5 percent and 2.5 percent. That inherently allows US real estate to experience more buying and selling cycles—a 2 percent closing cost does not have a large impact on the wallet, whereas a 10 percent closing cost in Europe is a significant part of the investment. In Europe, 10 percent makes you think twice about buying or selling (and once you sell, you usually buy again), so European sales cycles are longer. Over the span of twenty years, properties in the United States might see three or four different owners whereas in Europe there might only be one.

The closing costs in the United States vary from title company to title company, but traditionally there are three or four fees involved that allow your property to be recorded in the county where your property is located; these fees also provide you with a title insurance policy that protects your investment in the event of an issue with the title.

The dynamic sales cycle in the US is encouraging for investors; it lets you know that at any point in time, you might be able to sell your house. There will be interest in your property because there are buyers out there who aren't concerned about closing costs—they're just concerned about getting their hands on your property. That is one of the magical aspects of the US real estate market.

RESALE OF A PROPERTY

There's a tax of approximately 10 percent of the gross income from the resale of property owned for more than one year. This is higher (approximately 25 percent) if the property is sold within the first twelve months of purchase.

However, if you are thinking of reinvesting the profits on your sale in under six months, then Internal Revenue Code 1031 Exchange allows you to avoid taxation for as long as you are reinvesting those profits.

CONCLUSION

Fiscally speaking, there are a number of great reasons to invest in real estate. By viewing real estate as a business, the United States makes it easy to reduce your tax exposure.

We've talked about finding and rehabbing properties, the financial aspects of investing in real estate, and some specifics about the Section 8 program itself. Now let's look at other considerations in dealing with this type of housing.

CHAPTER 7 TAKEAWAYS

A large number of tax deductions are applicable on received income in the US, reducing taxable net income. Some of the more common tax-deductible business expenses claimed on tax returns include the following:

- advertising
- auto and travel expenses
- cleaning and maintenance
- commissions
- depreciation
- insurance
- legal and other professional fees
- management fees
- mortgage interest paid to banks
- repairs
- real estate taxes
- utilities

Land trusts provide a huge tax advantage for investors who want to set up a succession strategy that can optimize tax liability down the road.

CHAPTER 8

OTHER CONSIDERATIONS

We are exposed to all sorts of before-and-after television shows that make the renovation of a property look very pleasing and fulfilling. It can indeed be fulfilling, and it definitely takes the right people to have the vision and the know-how to create a finished product. When it comes to entry-level properties that have been abandoned for months and that require all sorts of work, it can be quite difficult to even know where to start.

After having renovated over five hundred single-family homes, I can say that patience is a key skill to have. The magic really comes when you pass that first inspection and see your tenants pull up with the moving truck to bring in their furniture and belongings.

My company has had houses that didn't even have a roof on them to begin with. That usually means that everything else will need to be addressed: drywall, windows, electrical, plumbing, air conditioning, and flooring. But entrepreneurship is all about turning around a nonperforming product.

In this chapter, we will discuss some additional key factors that can make or break your venture in the entry-level real estate market.

CITY PERMITS

If you are to start work on a distressed property, you usually will need a variety of city permits. You will typically be asked to pull structural, mechanical, electrical, and plumbing permits, which involves a whole series of people, from general contractors to city officials. But don't let this discourage you; with the right property management team, you can bring your property into compliance with the city.

The administrative aspect of the product—the paperwork, the follow-through, various meetings with the city—can keep you busy for months at a time and can keep you from reaching your final goal of having a tenant in your property. Seriously, I've watched cranes move in, floor after floor get built, and paint applied as the finishing touches to a building, all while I was still trying to get the electrical work done in a small, single-family house one-tenth the size of that neighboring structure.

Consequently, launching a Section 8 real estate venture is not something you should attempt on your own, especially if you have a full-time job. This is something that requires very high follow-through and delegation to clearly skilled people who need to be trusted to take a product to the inspection process.

THE SAFETY ISSUE

Section 8 inspectors check for safety issues before approving a house for occupancy. A Section 8 inspector is going to check all the electrical outlets to make sure that they're grounded and is going to check whether you have working ground fault interrupter (GFI) outlets in the bathrooms and kitchens. These kick off automatically if there's an overload of the socket, but GFI outlets don't guarantee that electrical panel wiring has been done correctly or that a breaker hasn't been overloaded and is on the verge of burning out.

If you're just looking at the cosmetics of a property, you're taking a risk. You may walk through and see that your handyperson has put the kitchen tile in and painted the walls, and you may see that the lights and the water faucets work. But that's not a good indicator of what the property is going to undergo when a family moves in and is using the stove, washing machine, air conditioner, and television all at the same time.

We've purchased properties and found them rewired in ways that were unbelievably unsafe. If it worked in the past, then you can leave it that way and pass housing inspection, but you're much better off getting an expert to look at those various issues. Even if it costs an extra $600 or $1,400 to redo an electrical panel, it's an expense that's better handled before a family moves in. It will provide you with peace of mind and allow your tenants to live in proper conditions for the long term. The moment your tenant calls you and says that half the house has no power, breakers are popping, or there are burned wires here and there, you're going to go into a bit of a panic mode—and you're going to have to reach for your checkbook.

As a management company, we're able to hire experts who can bring pieces of a project into compliance for Section 8 without necessarily needing permits. If you're an individual investor and you're going to rely on your handyperson to rewire a house, you have a 50/50 chance of finding the right person. Many handypeople say that they can do everything, but that's rarely the case. Usually they have some very good core skills, but they rarely have a mastery of everything. For instance, you wouldn't want to hire a painter to rewire a house—electricity is nothing to mess with, and it requires someone who knows what they're doing.

As an investor, you obviously want the cheapest solution to a problem, but it's also good to look at the worst-case scenario. If further damage or a really dramatic issue can occur down the road, then it's best to spend that extra money now.

At the end of the day, it's good to surround yourself with good people who have some experience that can reasonably guide you— people who will remind you, "Look, don't be so cheap about this. Take the steps to create a balanced investment that has longevity to it and allows the tenant to live in a safe way. You don't want to have a liability on your hands."

CONCLUSION

When dealing with Section 8 properties, there are some scenarios you want to be aware of or to avoid altogether. These include dealing with permits, being aware of safety, and protecting your property from theft and damage. But there are ways to reduce your exposure in most situations, and we'll talk a little about those in the next chapter.

CHAPTER 8 TAKEAWAYS

- When starting work on a distressed property, you will likely need structural, mechanical, electrical, and/or plumbing permits, the obtainment of which involves a whole series of people, from general contractors to city officials.
- Section 8 inspectors check for safety issues before approving a house for occupancy.
- A good property management company can help property managers obtain permits and prepare for safety inspections.

CHAPTER 9

REDUCING YOUR EXPOSURE

As a real estate investor, an important part of your business is protecting your assets. While most of us realize that property insurance is a must-have, liability insurance is an often-overlooked aspect of a risk management program. Liability insurance, including general liability (which protects against slips and falls) and directors and officers liability insurance (which protects against many other commercial liabilities), can be the number-one protector of your income and wealth. Without a proper liability insurance program, all the benefits of your investments can disappear because of lawsuits or other claims against you.

Rental properties are exposed to many risks. Tenants are capable of many unpredictable claims and accusations. In addition, guests of your tenants or neighborhood pets can also cause a disruption on your property and harm your residents.

The key is to understand that you can be held responsible for whatever anyone or anything does on your property. General liability insurance is very affordable and should always be considered to protect your investment. Policies typically have limits of liability up to $1 million, and costs start at about $500 per year for a small property, so it's a very wise expense to consider.

INSURANCE FOR RENTALS

As I've mentioned, a way to protect your capital is to form an LLC through which you purchase your property. An LLC is primarily designed to surround the property with a shell so that if there is litigation, it won't affect your other assets. So that's the first step of any risk-reduction strategy; every house that you purchase should have its own LLC.

The next best step is a general liability insurance policy. If you don't have a general liability insurance policy for a property and there's litigation that isn't defended, a judgment and a lien can be placed on that property, which encumbers the asset. And the day you sell it, that judgment has to be satisfied.

There are certain usual and customary exclusions in each of these policies—such as mold or dog bites—so you want to make sure to read through them carefully. You might find that the liability insurance actually does not cover some of the most crucial areas in which you feel you might need it. Swimming pools and garages are other exposures that sometimes have restrictive exclusions pertaining to them.

As a counterargument to liability insurance, if attorneys ask for your insurance information and you don't have any, many of them become discouraged and don't pursue action against you. The time and effort required to pursue and potentially get a judgment against you on your property could be in the thousands of dollars in terms of their time. So it's very possible that if you have no liability insurance, attorneys will discourage their clients from going forward in a lawsuit; they might instead try to work out a deal for some kind of settlement.

This is actually one of the arguments that some investors have used: they don't have insurance, because they feel that's what attorneys are looking for. Or if they pass a problem on to an insurance company, they argue, and then their insurance company could drop their policy because they have a claim.

I strongly recommend having liability insurance because the tenant population you're dealing with has few resources and any opportunity for a cash settlement is likely to be pursued with vigor. If and when there's an opportunity for them to press a claim for something, some of them might go to great lengths to obtain damages from you because they perceive you as having money; they'll just lean on an attorney whose job is to try to squeeze every drop out of you.

Any liability insurance policy has the potential to become cheaper as you grow your portfolio. For example, if you have three or four properties, instead of a $400 or $500 premium per property, you might have premiums of only a few hundred dollars per property. Having a portfolio can also give you access to commercial programs outside the traditional residential policies offered by many insurance companies.

Insurance is typically purchased outside of any contract with a management company, although some companies will research quotes for an investor. This is a handy service for overseas investors.

If you're considering an insurance policy, also check on the loss-of-rent benefits and see if they're worth considering.

FORMS OF RENTAL PROPERTY INSURANCE

Insurance for rental properties comes in several forms. The policies have various names, but some traditional ones are DP1, DP2, and DP3 (DP stands for *dwelling property*).

A DP1 policy is the most basic coverage and protects against acts such as fire and vandalism. It is an actual cash value policy, similar to a car insurance policy. As the property ages, it is worth less; therefore, any insurance claims will, over time, compensate you less to replace materials because the policy considers the materials to have depreciated over time. This is the key differentiator from a replacement cost policy, which is what DP2 and DP3 policies are.

The most common perils that are covered by a DP1 policy are fire, lightning, internal and external explosions, windstorms, hail, riot and civil commotion, smoke, aircraft and vehicles, volcanic explosion, vandalism, and malicious mischief.

A DP2 policy protects against the same perils as a DP1 policy (windstorms, hail, fire, vandalism, etc.), but in addition, it might also include coverage for things like: collision in case a car runs into the house, burglary damage, weight of ice and snow, glass breakage, accidental discharge or overflow of water or steam, falling objects, frozen pipes, electrical damage, or collapse. A DP2 policy is a replacement cost policy, which means that—unlike a DP1 policy—it does not deduct for depreciation.

A DP3 policy offers the most comprehensive coverage that can be obtained on rental properties. While DP1 and DP2 are "named" peril policies, DP3 is an open-peril policy that covers all possible perils. DP3 insurance is also a policy that insures at replacement cost rather than actual cash value. This means that no matter how old your property is, the policy will cover all costs necessary for repairs (after the deductible is paid).

Some exceptions exist with a DP3 policy, and standard exclusions are common. These exclusions can include earth movement, some or all types of water damage, neglect, war, intentional loss, some or all molds, ordinance or law, governmental action, power failure, and nuclear hazard.

Typically speaking, on an annual basis a DP1 policy costs about one month's rent, and a DP3 policy costs about one-and-one-half months' rent. Prices vary based on the size of the house and, to some degree, the age of the property.

Insurance can appear to be quite expensive if you look at it from the standpoint that it's going to take you almost two months of rent to pay for full coverage. And keep in mind that if there is an issue, you still have a deductible. Many people don't go into a full-coverage insurance policy; if there's a $5,000 deductible, you might be able to repair some pretty significant issues before reaching that deductible, and therefore you might just save on the expense of insurance premiums. The vast majority of investors tend to opt for a basic liability insurance policy.

Insurance is negotiable when you're a cash investor. If you're getting financing, you don't have a choice in the matter, and you have to go through specific insurance companies that are approved by your lender.

Depending on the location of the house, you might also look at how coverage applies for certain environmental factors. For example, Florida is considered to be in a hurricane zone, and the season for hurricanes goes from May to the end of October. But the perception that Florida is often the victim of severe hurricanes is false; Florida is actually rarely subject to major storms. There are, however, statewide and nationwide insurance companies that provide hurricane coverage. It is important to comprehend the conditions of those contracts. This type of coverage is very pricey, and it also has deductibles that require out-of-pocket payments regardless of the situation.

But every area of the world is exposed to certain environmental risks. California may have earthquakes and forest fires, the Midwest may have tornadoes, and the north may have huge snowstorms. Each investor needs to examine his or her own fears when it comes to investing to consider whether the worst-case-scenario is something to prepare for. It's really about your mentality and your risk tolerance.

NOTIFICATIONS ABOUT VIOLATIONS

Homeowners associations and regulated housing developments often enforce a considerable number of rules and regulations regarding a property's use and appearance. Although these strict rules apply more often to apartments and condominiums than to single-family homes, that doesn't mean that communities in which single-family homes exist do not also have clear rules and regulations.

Cities exist for a number of reasons. Among these reasons is the need to offer residents a quality of life. To do that, cities need to maintain a certain standard of living and continually work to improve at the municipal level. As part of this effort, homeowners have a duty to maintain their property to a certain standard, and the city takes note of this.

For example, if a tenant has a car with an expired tag or no tag parked for an extended period of time—or if it is parked on the lawn instead of in the driveway—the homeowner will be notified that this is a violation that they are responsible for fixing. It doesn't matter that it's the tenant's car. So obviously you, as the lessor and homeowner, have to get in touch with the tenant. The issue is that the city will also give you a deadline, and if that deadline is not met, there can be fines of $100 or even $1,000 per day!

Another problem that can occur with rental properties is landscaping. For example, if the grass dies, the city will want you to resod the property, requiring you to purchase a couple of pallets of grass. But who's going to water the new grass? Your tenant won't want the high water bill. The solution is to work with city inspectors to lay down mulch, gravel, or some other low-maintenance landscape option. Our company tries to do whatever we can to avoid laying down what essentially amounts to a brand new putting green for tenants who won't care to maintain it.

What it boils down to is that even though these houses are not in regulated communities with homeowners association fees, the city does police the area.

Also keep in mind that your tenants may behave in ways that don't please the neighbors, who may then report them to the city's code enforcement department. Once code enforcement gets involved, they'll notify you of everything: excessive trash, a broken mailbox, loose exterior wiring, a unpermitted fence, or the need to repaint the entire house. The list can be quite extensive—and expensive. And there are deadlines for fixing the violations.

A management company often has access to preferred pricing on items such as mulch or pallets of grass, and it typically has the crew to rapidly bring a property back into compliance—often within forty-eight hours. But whether you use a management company or are doing the repairs yourself, the key is to show the inspectors that you are fast and efficient.

In lower-income neighborhoods, where Section 8 properties sometimes are located, tenants may not be familiar with rules regarding use and appearance of the property they are renting. If their car breaks down or the tag expires, they may not have the money to resolve the issue, and the car can end up in the driveway or yard without a tag.

There are things of this nature that will expose you to certain warnings from the city. Each city has its different kind of policing; some are stricter than others. What's important to note is that if you don't manage the violations, you reach a point where you're actually getting fined.

These fines can be pretty scary, and unfortunately, they often show up when you're trying to resell the property. For example, we've seen an instance where a buyer was ready to purchase a property, and when the title company did a lien search it found a $73,000 fine for having high grass! At $100 per day, that's 730 days—for two years, someone was living in an overgrown jungle of a property. This can happen with long-distance lessors who don't have a reliable management system in place.

When this happens, the lessor (or management company) has to go to the local magistrate and negotiate with the city, which has to validate that the property is compliant. In the above example, the homeowner ended up paying a $2,000 settlement—a large reduction from the original fine but still a big amount of money gone to waste.

Again, the owner has nothing to do with the violation other than being the holder of the property. But because they can result in a fine, a prompt response is crucial in these situations.

CONCLUSION

As with any real estate investment, challenges exist when dealing with Section 8 tenants. But you can protect yourself with the appropriate amount and type of insurance. In addition, when it comes to maintaining a property to avoid fines, a management company can be your best friend.

CHAPTER 9 TAKEAWAYS

- Property owners can be held responsible for whatever anyone or anything does on their property; therefore, it's important to properly insure your investments against liability claims.
- Rental (or dwelling) property insurance policies are available in a variety forms and can protect property owners in the event of natural disaster or common perils.
- Property owners have a duty to maintain their property to a certain standard, and the city can issue warnings and fines if the property violates a city code or law.

CHAPTER 10

THE VALUE OF USING A MANAGEMENT COMPANY

Most people don't have the time to look for $100,000 investment properties to use for Section 8 tenants much less manage repairs, show the house to potential renters, and manage other aspects of being a lessor. Even fewer know a good handyperson who can help make such a property rentable.

That's where a property management company can be an advantage. It sounds obvious, but think of the freedom and peace that this can provide; you simply pass the baton to a company to handle all the issues for you.

There are many types of property management companies out there, so the key is to find the one that has expertise in the single-family home market that you are looking to invest in. This might take a bit of research; there are websites such as www.allproperty-management.com that can help guide you to the companies in your local area, and simply doing a Google search will provide you with several options in the area you are interested in.

Management companies are businesses; the only way they can stay in business is by charging property owners for different kinds of services. If you're an investor trying to make a good income off a property, why would you want to give that money to a management company? The decision is based predominantly on your goals and where you are located relative to your property or properties.

It's fair to say that most people who invest in properties are managing them themselves. But if you happen to live far from a potential investment, then having it managed is a no-brainer; it's a crucial part of your business plan.

For foreign investors, the value of using a management company is that they don't actually have to come to the United States to invest; the majority of our investors are able to invest without ever seeing their properties. However, investing in real estate through our programs means that you're able to combine business with leisure by taking a trip to deal with the transaction and then taking the family to Disney World or the Florida Keys. These expenses are deductible because you're qualified to fly once a year to the United States to see and manage your investment, which includes meeting with your property manager. If you live in the United States, your flight is obviously also part of your business expenses and will be tax deductible.

Once you've decided to use a management company, it's a matter of finding the right one.

WHAT TO LOOK FOR IN A MANAGEMENT COMPANY

As you can see, dealing with the Section 8 system is a complicated process. It took me many years to learn to navigate it well, but now I have a thriving business dedicated to helping other investors. So I speak from experience when I say I believe a management company needs to be good in three areas.

First, a management company must be good on the leasing side of the equation. How quickly and efficiently is it able to get a tenant into your property?

Second, a management company must have accurate accounting systems in place. This is crucial to your success as an investor and requires property management software that tracks basically two things: the tenants' ledgers and the owners' ledgers. Then anything that happens on a tenant's ledger must be transcribed onto the owner's ledger. It's vital for your accounting team to have the skill set to provide clarity in the ledgers. Too often, the statements to owners are so convoluted that they're impossible to understand. Fees and income are listed over here, expenses over there—nothing is clear, and it doesn't instill confidence about the investment. Most software now has cloud capability, so your investors can check on the performance of their properties at any time.

Third, a management company must be able to quickly and effectively repair properties. Can the company do repairs in a cost-effective way? Does it have the right resources? Does it have the right people? Does it have the ability to get the job done right the first time? When a management company gets big enough, its phones ring day and night with calls to fix leaky sinks, broken windows, or invasions of pests. All these things require efficient teams. If the management company gets a call for a plumbing issue, it usually outsources the service to a plumbing company and bills the cost to the owner of the property. But once a management company gets large enough, it can bring some of these services in-house and can ultimately lower the cost of repairs while having control over its staff's performance.

When considering management companies, get an understanding of the company's culture. Talk to the leasing agents to get an understanding of how strong the company's rental market is. Find out what kind of policies the company has in place regarding leases. Ask for a fee schedule. Ask for a sample statement. Ask about in-house services and what services are outsourced. Get an idea of the general costs for repairing an air conditioner, for cleaning a drain line, or for a standard plumbing repair.

HOW MANAGEMENT COMPANIES MAKE MONEY

Management companies make money in three ways: management fees, leasing fees, and markup fees. Oftentimes, management companies have the reputation of unnecessarily charging for everything. In truth, as a business, they often have significant expenses such as liability insurance, office space, worker's compensation, and payroll.

The most common fee that a management company will charge you is a percentage of the rents that they collect, which for most companies varies from 7 percent to 10 percent. The main reason you pay this management fee is to secure the rental income stated in your contract by using the company's expertise to manage the day-to-day needs of your tenant.

A property management company has leasing agents, and those agents have an array of contacts, databases, and resources to find tenants. This is their strength, and it allows you to get away from trying to find tenants yourself and spending time showing your property.

Once the management company places a tenant in your property, its basic role is to collect rent money for you and maintain your property. That's when you need a management company that understands collections and has the skill to build relationships with tenants.

Just as a management company's job is to get you tenants, to collect your rent, and to have the tools to fix your property, it also needs to be competent at getting your tenants out of your property when needed. As I mentioned earlier, that's why we employ eviction specialists.

With a management company, you also are paying for the benefit of never having to be on the phone with the tenant yourself. That gives you peace and extra time to benefit from your investment without being a twenty-four-hour hotline for tenants in need of repairs or who want permission to pay late. Our clients want to stay with us for the simple reason that we're there for them: we fix things that need to be fixed, and we always keep in mind that the tenants are the key to our success. Without the tenants, we are left with empty homes and empty bank accounts for the investors, which is not an environment that breeds high returns.

Second only to the management fee is the leasing fee. This one is pretty standard: A property management company has a brokerage license and therefore has the right to charge you up to a month of rent for leasing your property. When a real estate agent leases your house, they will usually take a payment for the first and last month's rent, along with a security deposit. Usually, one of those payments is going to go to the agent who found you the tenant, so it costs you one month of rent to find a tenant (in most cases). Management companies usually have a higher volume of properties to rent, so some of them are able to trim that fee down a little.

Some management companies have a different fee schedule when it comes to leasing fees and charge only half a month's rent, which is obviously better for your overall net income. In recent years, companies have also been charging a lease renewal fee when the tenant decides to stay in the property. This covers the time and effort involved in rewriting your lease and securing your tenant for another year. Typically, it involves redoing all the inspections, sending all the paperwork in again, revalidating, and so forth because there's an entirely new government contract. With a Section 8 tenant, the paperwork involved in leasing a property is almost the same every year as it is the first year, so lease renewal fees tend to be seen as a fair cost to incur; usually it's 25 percent of one month's rent. It's definitely better than losing your tenant, losing a month of rent, and enduring all the other preparation involved in renting your property again.

Markup fees are another main source of income for management companies; these are pretty normal for the industry as a whole. A management company needs maintenance staff for different trades, such as electricians, plumbers, air conditioning technicians, and pest control technicians. This system of maintenance staff is designed to provide quick and efficient service to your tenants so that your property doesn't deteriorate further and doesn't expose your tenant to a safety or health issue. Markup fees vary between companies; most charge a 10 percent markup on all work orders.

Management companies also benefit from actually having two customer bases—investors (like you) and tenants, who also provide the management company with a number of fees such as application fees, late fees, and pet fees. All these fees add up over time and are there to support the business and ultimately the property owner's income.

Some management companies charge you when one or more of your properties are vacant. These fees are generally for recurring maintenance needed when no one lives in the house, such as mowing the grass. The fees cover the people who actually handle this maintenance, but they also cover the administration costs (paperwork, record-keeping, etc.). If you are the investor, I strongly recommend avoiding these fees because they're just going to hinder your income. Just make sure that you only pay management fees when the property is occupied.

With any type of investment, higher return on investment requires higher management involvement and expertise. Higher returns inevitably involve a constantly moving and evolving product—in this case, tenants who are not as versed in maintaining a property, who are unable to obtain consistent work, or who have other financial difficulties. The management develops its expertise every day by working with this type of housing program and the general requirements that come with a federal program.

Section 8 exposes you to issues that you might not have when renting to a traditional family. But for my company, there is clear security in having steady rent come in between the first and third of the month, whether it is for our properties or for those that we manage for our investors.

CONCLUSION

After reading this book, you should now see what it takes to invest in real estate with very little money and to generate returns that far outperform all other investment channels. I've told you what it takes to be a different investor: one who thinks outside the box and is looking to beat the averages and obtain results that cannot be found anywhere besides the United States.

There can be headaches when dealing with acquisitions, closings, renovations, tenant placement, collections, and repairs, but using a property management company can eliminate those headaches. Issues happen with real estate at pretty much every price level, but in the low price range, you're dealing with a much higher level of competition. You need experts who have specific and privileged relationships with asset managers and banks, repairmen and suppliers, and housing officials and inspectors. From a business standpoint—one in which you can own high-performing rental properties without ever leaving your couch.

Finally, as I've mentioned several times, the key in this business is keeping your tenants. No one's going to be more qualified to help you do that than a skilled management company that earns its fees by stabilizing your assets and creating good customer service.

CHAPTER 10 TAKEAWAYS

- If you live far from a potential investment, then it makes good sense to hire a property management company.
- A property management company needs to be good in three areas:
    1. leasing

    2. accounting

    3. repairs

- Management companies make money in three ways:
    1. management fees

    2. leasing fees

    3. markup fees

ABOUT THE AUTHOR

Antoine Gendre emigrated to the US at an early age and completed his university studies at Florida State University. Since then, he has become an American citizen and has made it his mission to provide others around the world the chance to live the American dream—that of owning a home that contributes to wealth generation.

Somehow born with a great memory, Antoine has used his talent to remember every single house he has ever bought and sold to his clients, which allows him to stay close to their investments and needs.

Today, Antoine spends his time between Miami and Detroit where he and his wife oversee their real estate activities.

To learn more about real estate investment opportunities available today, visit ameristargroupe.com.

APPENDIX
A CONSUMER'S GUIDE TO INVESTING IN A SECTION 8 PROPERTY

HOW TO AVOID FOUR REAL ESTATE INVESTMENT RIP-OFFS

Rip-off #1: Unbelievably low prices. To some degree, all of us are attracted by low prices because we want to work within a budget. But some really cheap real estate can be very misleading. You can find a property for $30,000, but if it is in a really bad area, then nobody will want to rent from you, so you will end up with an asset that pays you nothing, even after renovations. Real estate investments need to be purchased in areas where families will be able to live safely; that is the criterion that your property search has to start with.

Rip-off #2: Illegal extensions. Some properties seem like great deals but are tagged by the city as having "open permits" or unpermitted extensions. Unfortunately, these situations are very difficult and costly to deal with and can turn your investment into a very unpleasant experience. You think you have a great four-bedroom house lined up, but then you find out that it's really a three-bedroom house with an extension that the previous owner did illegally. You will likely have to obtain several permits and tradespeople to complete the inspection process with the city, and you could be reaching deep into your pocket.

Rip-off #3: Unsupported claims. "Rents for $1,200/month." You'll often read this claim when looking for rented properties to purchase. Remember that the seller is looking to get rid of the property and is not looking out for your best interests. If you want to buy an already rented property, make sure to get a copy of the lease and the latest tenant ledger to ensure that the rent being advertised is accurate and that the tenant is paying it in full. The standard in real estate law is to request an estoppel letter from tenants to be certain of the lease details and payment history.

Rip-off #4: Outdated pictures. "Renovated and rent ready." Many people are shown pictures of properties that appear to be freshly painted and fully renovated. But in reality, those pictures are from three years ago, before tenants moved in. Today, it's a common practice to show buyers false and outdated pictures to make them pay top dollar. By visiting the property or asking someone to obtain recent pictures or videos, you will be able to get a much better idea of the overall property condition and the value of the investment.

SIX MISCONCEPTIONS ABOUT SECTION 8 INVESTMENTS

Misconception #1: Section 8 properties have specific characteristics and can't be found everywhere.

Not true. Any house, regardless of size or location, can be rented to Section 8 tenants as long as it falls within Section 8 criteria. That means providing a functional, safe, and clean property that allows a family to live in the same, normal conditions in which anyone would want to live.

Misconception #2: Section 8 tenants destroy your property.

Not true. Section 8 tenants are not necessarily risky tenants. The great majority are simply honest citizens who have qualified for Section 8 on account of their low income. More often than not, this type of tenant will be at least as careful as a tenant who receives no government aid. If you have broken windows, recurring plumbing issues, and other chronic maintenance issues, one major source of your problem could be insufficient screening of tenants and failing to get references from their previous lessor. These precautions are recommended for all prospective tenants, not just those in Section 8.

Misconception #3: Damage caused by Section 8 tenants will be covered by the PHA.

Not true. The PHA is not responsible for damage caused to your property and will ask you to execute your lease directly with your tenant. However, Section 8 reserves the right to reduce the value of the voucher or terminate it entirely if a tenant is clearly not respecting his or her tenancy contract. The most effective way to cover yourself is to obtain a strong security deposit and coordinate quarterly inspections of your property for regular maintenance. Keep in mind that the presence of multiple children means a lot of foot traffic around all areas of the property and repetitive usage of doors, windows, appliances, etc.

Misconception #4: Section 8 money is guaranteed.

Not true. Although you do enter into a twelve-month contract with a federal program, there is no guarantee that you will be paid the contracted amount on your lease for the next twelve months. Tenants, whose income is verified quarterly, can be taken off the program either for having sufficient income to support themselves or for having certain undeclared income. While the Section 8 program offers strong income security, it comes with a wide array of conditions that must all be met year-round.

Misconception #5: The PHA pays 100 percent of the rent.

Not true. Each family is provided a voucher amount based on income verification and certain calculations; the PHA can identify what portion of the rent will be covered by the federal program and what portion will have to be covered by the tenant. The only time the government pays the entire rent is when the tenant does not work, so collecting your tenant's portion is part of your monthly requirements.

Misconception #6: Section 8 contracts are only valid for twelve months, and then you have to find a new family to rent your property.

Not true. Housing contracts are indeed twelve months in length, but a vast majority of tenants renew their leases and stay for many years. The average time that a tenant stays in a property is an unpredictable figure, and there are several factors that either force the family to leave or allow the family to remain in the property for many years. Three things can cause your tenant to decide to move after only twelve months:

1. You are not maintaining your property, and the tenant has found a freshly painted and renovated property to move to. Other lessors are eager to rent their properties and create direct competition with you, so you should cater to your tenants' needs if you want to keep them.

2. The tenant made too quick of a decision when moving to your property and doesn't like the area, fears break-ins, or fears that the kids will be hanging with the wrong crowds. A property in an undesirable area will see more turnover and be exposed to more vandalism when it is vacant.

3. The utilities at the property are too high, and the tenant wants to find a more energy-efficient house or a house where there is less space to heat or cool (depending on the climate and time of year). If you add insulation or install energy-efficient systems, you might have a better chance to keep your tenant for longer.

WHICH TYPE OF HOUSE IS BEST?

Number of bedrooms: A three-bedroom house or larger has the advantage of hosting a family in a spacious area and allowing members of the family to have their own areas of privacy and usage of the house. It's also a wise choice if you want to resell the house. A house that only has two bedrooms is ideal for a couple, but as soon as the couple wants to expand their family, they need a bigger house.

Single-family houses: The single-family house allows you to stay away from condominium associations and rental restrictions that come with various communities. The unpredictable administrative issues that can come with living in a regulated community can seriously affect your ability to rent your property and thus your cash flow. Moreover, association fees eat into your net return on investment.

Some people believe that having a rental property in a nice, gated community is a safe investment. Besides the risk of being exposed to unexpected changes in monthly fees, you also run the risk of being the victim of strict policy changes. Associations can decide that you are not allowed to rent for the first year after you purchase. They might decide that they wish to rent to only a specific income bracket or minimum credit score. Or they might decide to limit the number of parking spots for residents or guests. All these possibilities can affect your net return on investment and provide you with headaches and a feeling of being trapped within a system and a board of directors. Being an investor is like running a business. Putting yourself in the hands of a homeowners association is like having an unpredictable business partner who takes a share of the profits every month.

Residences near schools: This is a way to keep tenants in your home for a while. Section 8 families are always looking for their kids to be near a school. If their kids are within walking distance of the school, you are certain to have a tenant who stays for a while—often until all the children have graduated from that establishment.

Number of bathrooms: Parents always enjoy having their own bathrooms; it's no different with Section 8. A second bathroom allows the adult(s) to have their privacy and use of an independent bathroom while the children share a common bathroom. We also recommend that one of the bathrooms be equipped with a bathtub rather than a standup shower. Section 8 families often have young babies, and a bathtub provides the ideal conditions for bathing a young toddler. In certain geographical areas such as Detroit, a majority of homes are only equipped with one bathroom, so the selection is predominantly focused on the number of bedrooms.

Tile floors: Electing to install tile floors is a money-saving decision that will keep you away from yearly carpet cleaning or carpet replacements. Can you imagine a family of five running in and out of a rental property that is covered with carpet? Tile floors are easy to clean, more hygienic, and much more cost-effective for an investor. If you purchase a house that has carpet, replace it with tile. Tile is an investment that will pay off several times over.

EIGHT MISTAKES TO AVOID WHEN CHOOSING A PROPERTY MANAGEMENT COMPANY

Mistake #1: Choosing a property manager based on his or her claim to be able to lease your property fast.

There is no question that your property management company needs to fill your property with a tenant. But it also needs something else. It needs employees who are skilled at holding tenants accountable to their leases. Many companies lease units all day long, but very few companies teach their leasing agents how to enforce the lease throughout its entire term. This requires providing the right balance between protecting the owner's interest and taking the necessary steps to retain the tenant and provide for his or her needs. The best way to know that a property manager's leasing agents have been properly trained is to make sure that the leasing agent is a certified realtor or has a community association management (CAM) license. Before you use a property manager, ask to see updated proof of the company's certification and the leasing agent's certification.

Mistake #2: Choosing a property manager based on low prices or management fees.

Low management fees could be a problem in three ways. First, low price can be the bait that attracts your phone call, but once the property is in your manager's hands, you are pressured into a much higher cost of management. Second, low management fees can mean that a limited number of services are offered. Third, low management fees can mean that the property manager has few resources (such as software, plumbers, electricians, and accurate accounting staff) to manage your property well. The latter two of these issues could result in you having to hire your own accountants, contractors, etc.

Mistake #3: Choosing a property manager based on a single telephone call.

Instead, request to visit a property that the company has renovated to lease, and ask for a written estimate of what was done to the property. Then you'll know exactly what the manager suggests renovating before renting the property, and you won't be the victim of continuous add-ons and unpredictable bills that escalate in front of your eyes.

Mistake #4: Choosing a property manager who doesn't offer a money-back guarantee.

In my view, property managers should be fully accountable for their work, and if you end up with a bad tenant, you shouldn't have to pay for it—period. Not all property managers offer a guarantee, or if they do, the guarantee may be "limited." Ask the property management company if it offers a money-back guarantee, and then make sure the property management company includes its guarantee in its management contract.

Mistake #5: Choosing a property manager without getting comments from his or her existing clients.

Any property manager can say anything about their past performance, and sadly, some of what they say may not be true. Make sure to ask for references or read comments from current customers to determine if you can depend on the property manager and their work.

Mistake #6: Choosing a property management company that isn't certified with a local real estate board.

If your property manager isn't a close friend, you may not know whether he or she has the knowledge or experience to manage properties well. If you want to make sure you're hiring a competent professional, make sure the company has a real estate license. The property managers must earn their certification through study, experience, and successful completion of formal examinations. In effect, licensed property managers have earned a college degree in property management.

Mistake #7: Choosing a property manager who hasn't obtained a brokerage license.

Holding a brokerage license is for property managers who are dedicated to the following:

1. Honest, ethical business practices
2. Staying current on the latest compliance laws for property management, leasing, and evictions
3. The highest possible protection of your rents through a trust account

You're making a wise decision when you have your property managed by licensed brokers.

Mistake #8: Choosing a property manager who doesn't use a cloud-based property management software. You might expect this from me, as my employees and I use this type of software. But there are several good reasons for using this kind of technology. Excel spreadsheets and QuickBooks are good, but they aren't as good as property management software, and cloud-based property management software is the Rolls Royce of property management software. Cloud-based property management software uses accessible, specific real estate accounting and data fields, so throughout the management of your property, you get much better feedback and clarity on the performance of your property—no two ways about it.

THE IMPORTANCE OF VALUE AND PRICE

Price is what you pay. Value is what you get.

When you select a property manager, you'll choose from a wide variety of management methods and prices. I recommend working with a property management company that specializes in Section 8 if you decide that you want to rent to a Section 8 tenant. A property management company that specializes in Section 8 manages much more than a standard residential management company for three reasons:

1. It has much more experience in dealing with the paperwork and the yearly requirements that come with renting to Section 8. In order for a tenant to move into your property, many things have to happen, and Section 8 specialists are essential in getting your tenants in and doing what's best to keep them there for the long term.

2. It allows you to get the optimal rent from your property. Section 8 specialists know the local voucher amounts that the government is willing to pay based on the number of bedrooms that the property has. Therefore, your Section 8 specialists will create the highest income possible for you.

3. Section 8 pays homeowners higher rent amounts than traditional tenants pay. However, in order to get those higher rents, you have to comply with many requirements or you will be penalized with an abatement (the suspension of your payments for noncompliance). A Section 8-specialized firm is ideally positioned to avoid such events.

Not surprisingly, using a property management company that specializes in Section 8 costs more than a property management company that rents to traditional tenants. If you bought an investment property to receive Section 8 tenants, then hiring a realtor might be all you need. There is no question that it will allow you to get some of the results you were looking for—but the key word here is "some." The realtor will not have the infrastructure to handle pre-inspections, inspections, collection protocols, lessor packages, and service calls.

On the other hand, if you want your Section 8 investment property to perform optimally and give you the best return on investment possible, then you need to hire a property management company that specializes in Section 8. Such a firm should have the infrastructure and trained staff in place to stay in compliance with governmental requirements and to oversee the many details required to receive rent year-round.

WHY YOU WANT A WELL-MANAGED SECTION 8 PROPERTY

Which is more important to you: a Section 8 tenant renting your house or a happy Section 8 tenant living in your house? Yes, I assure you, there is a difference.

Each property management method has advantages and disadvantages. Some methods will get you the rents. Other methods will get you the rents and handle the paperwork. Still others will do virtually everything for you. And, to be sure, some are more expensive than others.

If all you want is cheap, basic property management—which you might be able to do yourself or you might be able to find a realtor to manage your properties for 6 percent of gross rents—then I respectfully ask that you call another company.

But if you want to protect your wallet, if you want to protect your investment in real estate, if you want to protect your family from the stress of continuous repairs and maintenance issues that you have to get involved with, then you're invited to call me.

Property management companies that specialize in Section 8 are the most effective in optimizing your rental property's income. It's one of the most expensive services on the market, but we specialize in Section 8 for a good reason. More and more investors want the security that Section 8 can provide and its higher income possibilities.

Have you ever seen how some people are always looking for bills or receipts when tax time comes? If you have, then you know that you can pile up a lot of invoices that are spread around between unlabeled folders and messy desks. If you want your taxes done right, you can scan them all into cloud-based property management software, and when it comes to tax time, you'll know where all your invoices and bills are.

The same is true for your property management strategy. You can hire a property manager for 5 percent of your gross rental income who will keep your bills "somewhere" and make you think that the books are going to be accurate. Or, if you want the job done right, I'll manage your property's profit-and-loss statement with state of the art, cloud-based software, and you'll *know* it's accurate.

So if you want a highly accurate year-end report, if you're willing to invest in protecting your time and your confidence, you're invited to call us. You'll receive a written estimate at no cost or obligation. And if you give us the go-ahead, you're further protected with our…

100 PERCENT NO-RISK GUARANTEE

We want you to be pleased—absolutely delighted, in fact—with every property that we manage for you, so every property comes with our ironclad, risk-free guarantee. What does that mean? Simply that if you aren't happy with our work, we'll repair and/or re-rent your property for free. And if you still aren't pleased, you pay nothing. Many companies don't guarantee their work, but we feel that nothing is more important than your complete and total satisfaction. We stand behind every job, 100 percent. If you ever have any questions or concerns about our work, please call us right away.

FOUR STEPS TO A WELL-MANAGED SECTION 8 INVESTMENT PROPERTY

If you're thinking of investing in Section 8 rental properties, we encourage you to follow these four steps:

Step #1: Make a commitment to yourself to get your property rented through the Section 8 program. The longer you wait, the less income you will be obtaining from your investment.

Step #2: List your objectives. Do you want to receive rents from a traditional tenant, by renting your property yourself, or hiring a realtor? Or do you want the extra income, government-backed program, and hands-off property management that we specialize in? Do you want to work with an honest, reputable company, or do you want to work with the cheapest property management company or realtor, not knowing if they will be in business tomorrow or have sufficient infrastructure in place to secure your income?

Step #3: Ask questions. The way to learn about a company is to ask specific questions and listen carefully to the answers. Here are eight tough questions to ask a property manager before you begin investing in a rental property:

1. What kind of property do you recommend?
2. What kind of tenants do you focus on?
3. What will your management team do to maintain my property?
4. How often will you inspect my property?

5. What training does your staff have in Section 8 requirements?
6. Do you use cloud-based property management software?
7. Are you a certified broker?
8. Are your leasing agents licensed realtors?

Step #4: Once you're satisfied that you're working with an honest, competent professional, ask for a standard property management contract. A management contract gives you the assurance that the company covers every part of the management needs of rental properties and lays out the costs, so there are no surprises.

By following these four steps, you'll gain all the information you need to make an informed, intelligent decision. If you want a quick, cheap property manager, many realtors on the Internet can help you. Or you can pick up a lease contract at Office Depot, buy a few tools from Home Depot, and do the management yourself.

But if you want your investment property to perform in a profitable, hands-free way—with Section 8 payments secured, regular inspections, tenant relations managed, and fast response to repair needs—then we invite you to call us.

We'll be happy to answer your questions, provide you with a ballpark cost estimate over the telephone, or go to your rental property and give you a free written quotation without cost or obligation of any kind.

To reach us, call 954-530-1337 or
visit ameristargroupe.com.
We look forward to hearing from you!

Printed in the USA
CPSIA information can be obtained
at www.ICGtesting.com
JSHW012054140824
68134JS00035B/3427